Great Child Illustrators
1880-1930

Darrell Heppner

Schiffer Publishing Ltd®

4880 Lower Valley Road, Atglen, PA 19310 USA

Dedication

To Anne Heppner (1938 to 2001)
My wife Anne loved to read a good book. She read for enjoyment and entertainment. After a nine year battle with breast cancer, Anne passed away at home in December of 2001. This book is dedicated to you, my dear.
—Darrell Heppner, 2003

Library of Congress Cataloging-in-Publication Data

Heppner, Darrell.
  Great children's illustrators / by Darrell Heppner.
    p. cm.
  ISBN 0-7643-1947-7 (pbk.)
  1. Illustrators. 2. Baby books--United States--History. I. Title.
NC975 .H45 2004
741.6'42'0973—dc22

2003027061

Designed by Mark David Bowyer
Type set in Shelley Allegro BT/Souvenir Lt BT

ISBN: 0-7643-1947-7
Printed in China
1 2 3 4

Published by Schiffer Publishing Ltd.
4880 Lower Valley Road
Atglen, PA 19310
Phone: (610) 593-1777; Fax: (610) 593-2002
E-mail: Info@schifferbooks.com

For the largest selection of fine reference books on this and related subjects, please visit our web site at
www.schifferbooks.com
We are always looking for people to write books on new and related subjects. If you have an idea for a book please contact us at the above address.

This book may be purchased from the publisher.
Include $3.95 for shipping.
Please try your bookstore first.
You may write for a free catalog.

In Europe, Schiffer books are distributed by
Bushwood Books
6 Marksbury Ave.
Kew Gardens
Surrey TW9 4JF England
Phone: 44 (0) 20 8392-8585; Fax: 44 (0) 20 8392-9876
E-mail: info@bushwoodbooks.co.uk
Free postage in the U.K., Europe; air mail at cost.

Contents

Introduction

Book collecting is an enjoyable hobby. For me, the world of illustrated children's books, including old baby books, is a never ending source of entertainment and joy. There are always new discoveries to be made.

As a child, I had books that my mother read to me. As an adult, I often thought about these books and toys of my childhood. A few years ago, I began to collect old illustrated children's books from the 1900 to 1940 period.

I found comfort in collecting particular illustrators. New illustrators continue to be found today; now there are books, calendars, and prints.

Among the books I had as a child were several by Johnny Gruelle, including *Little Brown Bear*, published by P. F. Volland & Company. As I began collecting, I discovered other beautiful books by P. F. Volland & Company. The selection of illustrators was exceptional and the books were of high quality printing and binding. Some were still in the original publisher's box. In one purchase I acquired a Volland baby book. Then I remembered that I had my own baby book packed away in a box of family photographs. My baby book was by Gibson & Company from the early 1930s.

As time went on, I began to acquire a few more baby books. Several book dealers who specialize in illustrated children's books searched their inventories and brought forth many interesting finds.

More than half the baby books in the collection have information about an actual baby contained within them. Since one of my other hobbies is family history and family genealogical research, this has been of particular interest to me. It has been a delightful adventure reading a mother's notes from a hundred years ago or thumbing through pages of baby and family photographs pasted in the book, along with hair and birthday and Christmas tags.

One of my goals is to reunite the baby books with the descendants of the children chronicled within. To date, I have sold one baby book to the great nephew of a lady who was born in the 1920s in New England. It made a wonderful addition to their box of family history. I hope that more of these baby books find their way to the current family of the baby whose book was published between 1880 and 1930. If you have information to share, I can be contacted at P.O. Box 958, San Leandro, California 94577 or via e-mail at Darrellrix@aol.com.

Chapter One

Baby Books: Fifty Wonderful Years: 1880-1930

One of the most delightful of works illustrated by children's artists of the late nineteenth and early twentieth centuries was the baby book. A baby book is a gift book in which the mother (we presume that in most cases mothers did the recording of their babies' information) records dates and events of a baby as he or she grows into childhood. However, baby books have no set format, no mandated topics. The author, illustrator, and publisher have a creative free hand in the design of the book. The results, as you will see, allow for imaginative topics and many beautifully decorated pages.

Some baby books have almost no space for dates, events, and notes. Others have large pages with lines and lines of writing space waiting to be filled in by the parent.

Some baby books are small in size and some are large format books. Some have less than a dozen pages; others are over fifty pages in length. Some baby books have soft covers that have survived the journey; others have heavy durable coverings.

During my research process, I discovered that certain lists of books compiled by author or by illustrator included a baby book along with their other publications.

In 1917, P. F. Volland & Company printed a sixteen page booklet promoting its array of beautiful books for children and gift books for adults. One of the books offered by Volland was *My Baby's Book*, 1915, by Ella Dolbear Lee and Julia Hardy with decorations by Ella L. Brison. Here is Volland's 1917 promotion for this book:

A Charming Gift Book. So often no record is kept of the interesting events of a Baby's life – when it first crept – when it stood alone – when it cut its first tooth, etc. And it is always a matter of deep regret for fathers and mothers who have neglected to keep such a record. That is why "My Baby's Book" is such a practical and appropriate gift to parents. It is compiled along new and original lines. Pages have been set apart and designated by appropriate titles and description for all the interesting and valuable information that should be kept about "Baby." Bound in Boards. Price $1.00 each. Bound in pink or blue moiré silk. Price $1.50 each." (*A Complete List of Volland Book Publications*, 1917.)

Some baby books have health tips for the baby and the mother included, especially those published after 1915.

And, if you happen to be interested in business advertisements from the 1900 to 1930 period, you will find certain baby books a new source for you to investigate. Advertisements for local businesses are found in some baby books along with national products for the baby and the family. *The Book of Baby Mine* by Melcena Burns Denny is an excellent example of this, with a specific city per book in some cases.

In 1917, the P. F. Volland Company issued *The New Complete List of Volland Book Publication*, a sixteen page colorful promotion of its books which were available. On page 8, Volland offers a choice of three covers for *My Baby's Book*, available in dark pink, light pink, or medium blue. Booklet, $250-350.

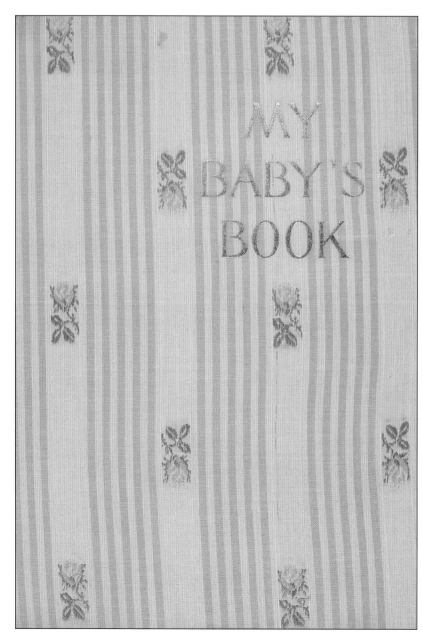

The cover of *My Baby's Book*, 1915, by Ella Dolbear Lee and Julia Dyar Hardy with illustrations by Ella L. Brison, published by P. F. Volland Company. This edition was bound in fabric with pink and white stripes and small pink roses. Book, $175-400.

Some baby books contain little information about their origin. This is the cover of *Baby* in blue silk, c. 1916, with neither author, illustrator, nor publisher denoted. Delicate fabric cover with the baby and title hand painted. Book, $75-125.

"When the LORD reached down His hand,
To add this Babe to our household band,
We felt that our cup must overflow,
The greatest blessing He could bestow."

"The Baby," another illustration from *Baby Days*, 1880, by Amy Neally and illustrated by Ida Waugh, Eddie Andrews, and Harriett M. Bennett, published by Dutton & Co., New York.

Baby and cherubs, frontispiece from *Baby Days*, 1880, by Amy Neally and illustrated by Ida Waugh, Eddie Andrews, and Harriett M. Bennett, published by Dutton & Co., New York. An example of the charming illustrations found in baby books of the late nineteenth and early twentieth centuries. Book, $100-250.

Chapter Two

The Illustrators of Baby Books

The authors and illustrators of baby books range from the famous to the anonymous. If you are a collector of illustrated children's books, you will be familiar with these names: Anne Anderson, Frances Brundage, Clara Burd, Fanny Cory, Bessie Pease Gutmann, Maud Humphrey, Henrietta Willebeeck Le Mair, Jessie Wilcox Smith, and Ida Waugh each illustrated or authored one or more baby books.

The 1880 to 1930 period was a time when artists, authors, and illustrators could make a modest to very good living on their artwork. Many of our baby book illustrators did work for many different publishers and a whole array of media, including books, magazine covers, postcards, calendars, commercial advertisements, etc.

This chapter contains brief biographical sketches of twelve authors and/or illustrators along with beautiful examples of their works. In addition, we have included in alphabetical order the other illustrators of baby books for whom we do not have biographical information.

Anne Anderson

In 1874, Anne Anderson was born to Scottish Lowland parents. Her childhood was spent in Argentina; she then lived in Berkshire. She married Alan Wright, with whom she collaborated on several children books. Anderson's decorative illustrations are in delicate color as well as black and white. Her illustrations display children in dress of the day with wonderful innocent faces. On both sides of the Atlantic, she was a very popular illustrator during the 1920s. She also did etchings, watercolors, and designed greeting cards. Her baby book is *Baby's Record,* issued in 1920 and reissued in 1928.

"Lullaby," an illustration from *Baby's Record,* (1920) 1928, by Anne Anderson, published by George Harrop & Co., England. Book, $125-250.

"Baby's First Step," an illustrated page from
Baby's Record, (1920) 1928, by Anne Anderson,
published by George Harrop & Co., England.

"Baby's Playmate," an illustration from *Baby's
Record,* (1920) 1928, by Anne Anderson, published
by George Harrop & Co., England.

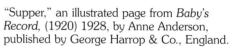

"Supper," an illustrated page from *Baby's Record*, (1920) 1928, by Anne Anderson, published by George Harrop & Co., England.

"Baby's Welcome," an illustrated page from *Baby's Record*, (1920) 1928, by Anne Anderson, published by George Harrop & Co., England.

"The Stork," frontispiece, from *Baby's Record*, (1920) 1928, by Anne
Anderson, published by George Harrop & Co., England.

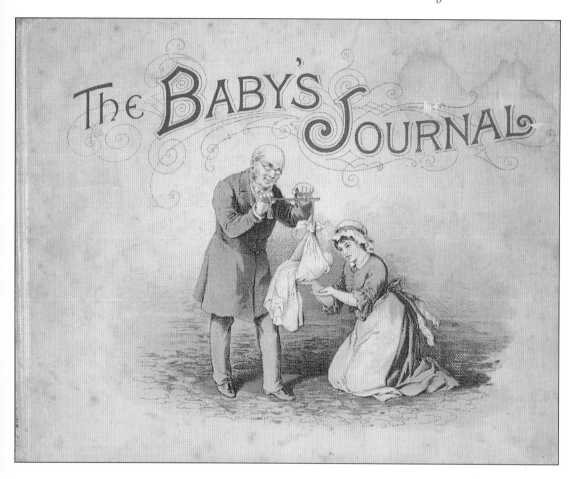

Illustrated cover with doctor and nurse weighing the baby from *The Baby's Journal*, 1883, by S. Alice Bray, published by Anson D. F. Randolph & Co., New York. Book, $50-150.

Decorated cover in brown leather from *The Baby's Journal*, 1885, by S. Alice Bray, published by Anson D. F. Randolph & Co., New York. Book, $50-150.

Blue cover of *The Baby's Journal*, c. 1900, by S. Alice Bray, published by Anson D. F. Randolph & Co., New York. Book, $50-150.

A light colored cover of *The Baby's Journal*, c. 1890, by S. Alice Bray, published by Anson D. F. Randolph & Co., New York. Book, $50-150.

Title page from *The Baby's Journal,* 1883, by S. Alice Bray, published by Anson D. F. Randolph & Co., New York.

"Weighing the Baby," an illustrated page from *The Baby's Journal,* 1883, by S. Alice Bray, published by Anson D. F. Randolph & Co., New York.

"Morning Bath," an illustration from *The Baby's Journal,* 1883, by S. Alice Bray, published by Anson D. F. Randolph & Co., New York.

Mother rocking baby in cradle, an illustrated page from *The Baby's Journal,* 1883, by S. Alice Bray, published by Anson D. F. Randolph & Co., New York.

"Oft in the Stilly Night," an illustrated page from *The Baby's Journal,* 1883, by S. Alice Bray, published by Anson D. F. Randolph & Co., New York.

"Learning to Walk," an illustration from *The Baby's Journal,* 1883, by S. Alice Bray, published by Anson D. F. Randolph & Co., New York.

"Puzzled," an illustrated page from *The Baby's Journal*, 1883, by S. Alice Bray,
published by Anson D. F. Randolph & Co., New York.

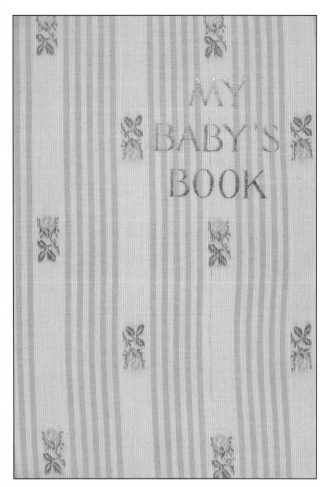

Fabric cover from *My Baby's Book*, 1915, by Ella Dolbear Lee and Julia Handy with illustrations by Ella L. Brison, published by P. F. Volland Co., Chicago. Book, $175-400.

Title page from *My Baby's Book*, 1915, by Ella Dolbear Lee and Julia Handy with illustrations by Ella L. Brison, published by P. F. Volland Co., Chicago.

MY BABY'S BOOK

A RECORD OF INTERESTING AND IMPORTANT EVENTS

Tattered book jacket from *My Baby's Book,* 1915, by Ella Dolbear Lee and Julia
Handy with illustrations by Ella L. Brison, published by P. F. Volland Co., Chicago.

Frances Brundage was one of many prolific American illustrators. She was a highly respected artist in her own time. Her style is easily recognized in her portrayal of adorable children and their household pets.

As described in *A Bit of Brundage,* by Sarah Steier and Donna Braun (Schiffer Publishing, 1999), her professional career began when she sold a sketch illustrating one of Louisa May Alcott's poems to the author. She subsequently illustrated over two hundred books during her career, the majority of them children's books. She also illustrated calendars, paper dolls, postcards, prints, trade cards, valentines, etc.

Brundage illustrated ten different baby books under several titles. They include *Baby, Baby's Book, Baby's Biography, Baby's Souvenir,* and *Our Baby.* Some books were done in collaboration with A. O. Kaplan, her husband Will Brundage, May Sandheim, and Ida Scott Taylor.

Blue and tan cover with embossed gilt lettering and embossed red balloon, *The Baby's Biography,* 1891, by A. O. Kaplan and illustrated by Frances Brundage, published by Brentano's, New York. Book, $150-300.

Red and tan cover with dark blue embossed balloon, *The Baby's Biography*, 1891, by A. O. Kaplan and illustrated by Frances Brundage, published by Brentano's, New York. Book, $150-300.

Embossed cover with red balloon, *The Baby's Biography*, 1891, by A. O. Kaplan and illustrated by Frances Brundage, published by Brentano's, New York. Book, $150-300.

Frontispiece from *The Baby's Biography,* 1891, by A. O. Kaplan and illustrated by Frances Brundage, published by Brentano's, New York.

Down the bright-hued Rainbow,
Straight from Heaven above;
Glides the new-born Infant
    Harbinger of Love.
Angels guard the pathway,
  Cherubs wave good cheer,
Mortals wait with greeting,
    Darling BABY DEAR.

"Merry Christmas Eve" page from *The Baby's Biography,* 1891, by A. O. Kaplan and illustrated by Frances Brundage, published by Brentano's, New York.

"Baby Was Given Its First Outing" page from *The Baby's Biography*, 1891, by A. O. Kaplan and illustrated by Frances Brundage, published by Brentano's, New York.

"Baby offered up its first Prayer" page from *The Baby's Biography*, 1891, by A. O. Kaplan and illustrated by Frances Brundage, published by Brentano's, New York.

Horseshoe for good luck wish for other folks' babies, an illustrated page from *The Baby's Biography*, 1891, by A. O. Kaplan and illustrated by Frances Brundage, published by Brentano's, New York.

Pale blue cover with pink and gold flowers, *Baby's Book,* c. 1900, by Ida Scott Taylor and illustrated by Frances Brundage, published by Raphael Tuck & Sons, London. Book, $150-300.

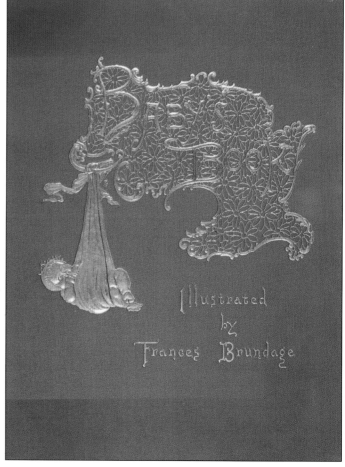

Deep blue cover with embossed gold lettering, *Baby's Book,* c. 1900, by Ida Scott Taylor and illustrated by Frances Brundage, published by Raphael Tuck & Sons, London. Book, $150-300.

Illustrated frontispiece with three baby faces from *Baby's Book*, c. 1900, by Ida Scott Taylor and illustrated by Frances Brundage, published by Raphael Tuck & Sons, London.

"First Word," an illustrated page from *Baby's Book*, c. 1900, by Ida Scott Taylor and illustrated by Frances Brundage, published by Raphael Tuck & Sons, London.

Decorated title page from *Baby's Souvenir*, c. 1910, by A. O. Kaplan with illustrations by Frances Brundage, published by Dean & Sons, London.

Silk cover with gold lettering, *Baby's Souvenir*, c. 1910, by A. O. Kaplan with illustrations by Frances Brundage, published by Dean & Sons, London. Book, $200-400.

"Merry Christmas Day," an illustration from *Baby's Souvenir*, c. 1910, by A.O. Kaplan with illustrations by Frances Brundage, published by Dean & Sons, London.

Title page with lovely decorations from *Our Baby*, 1903, by Frances Brundage and Will Brundage, published by C. R. Gibson & Co., New York. Book, $150-250.

First prayer page from *Baby's Souvenir*, c. 1910, by A. O. Kaplan and illustrated by Frances Brundage, published by Dean & Sons, London.

Rock-a-bye baby page from *Our Baby*, by Frances Brundage and Will Brundage, 1903, published by C. R. Gibson & Co., New York.

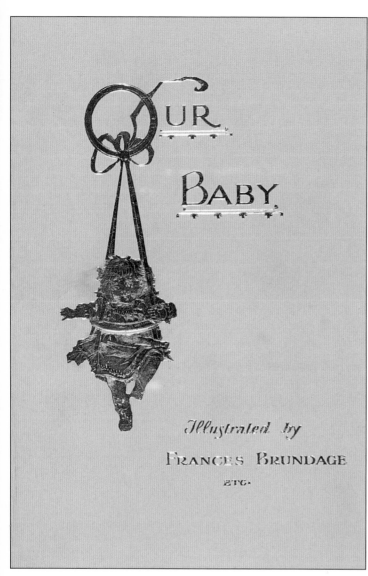

Light blue cover with silver and black lettering, *Our Baby*, 1909, by Frances Brundage and May Sandheim, published by Raphael Tuck & Sons, London. Book, $150-250.

Decorated title page from *Our Baby*, 1909 by Frances Brundage and May Sandheim, published by Raphael Tuck & Sons, London.

Only two cherry lips,
One chubby nose;
Only two little hands,
Ten little toes.

Only a golden head,
Curly and soft;
Only a tongue that wags
Loudly and oft.

"Only two cherry lips…," an illustrated page from *Our Baby*, 1909, by Frances Brundage and May Sandheim, published by Raphael Tuck & Sons, London.

Angel holding baby, an illustrated page from *Our Baby*, 1909, by Frances Brundage and May Sandheim, published by Raphael Tuck & Sons, London.

From the shining courts of Heaven,
One wee darling, pink and white!
Did you hear the cloud-gates open,
In the stillness of the night?
Did you hear a rush and flutter—
As if wings were plumed for flight?

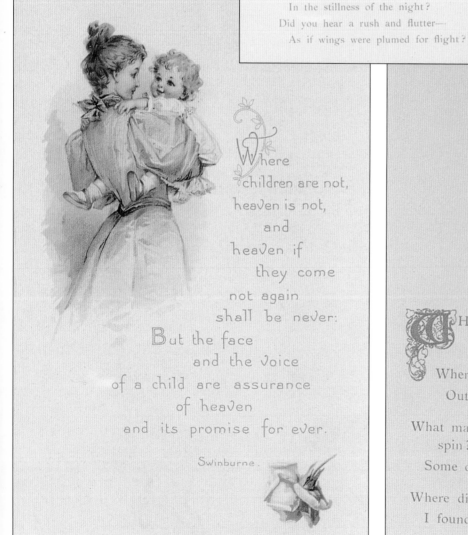

Where
children are not,
heaven is not,
and
heaven if
they come
not again
shall be never:
But the face
and the voice
of a child are assurance
of heaven
and its promise for ever.

Swinburne.

"Where children are not…," an illustrated page with verse from *Our Baby*, 1909, by Frances Brundage and May Sandheim, published by Raphael Tuck & Sons, London.

BABY.

WHERE did you come from, Baby dear?
Out of the everywhere into here.

Where did you get those eyes so blue?
Out of the sky as I came through.

What makes the light in them sparkle and spin?
Some of the starry spikes left in.

Where did you get that little tear?
I found it waiting when I got here.

Baby poem with illustration from *Our Baby*, 1909, by Frances Brundage and May Sandheim, published by Raphael Tuck & Sons, London.

THE BATH.

Only a golden head,
      Curly and soft ;
Only a tongue that wags
      Loudly and oft.

"The Bath," an illustrated page with poem from *Our Baby,* 1909, by Frances
Brundage and May Sandheim, published by Raphael Tuck & Sons, London.

FIRST STEPS.

There babbles from chair to chair
A sweet little face
That's a gleam in the place,
With its little gold curls of hair.

BENNETT.

"First Steps" illustration with poem from *Our Baby*,
1909, by Frances Brundage and May Sandheim,
published by Raphael Tuck & Sons, London.

Head of

flaxen

ringlets ;

Eyes of

Heaven's

blue ;

Parted

mouth—

a rosebud—

Pearls just

peeping

through.

Four babies' faces, illustration with poem from *Our Baby*, 1909, by Frances Brundage and May Sandheim, published by Raphael Tuck & Sons, London.

Clara Miller Burd was famous for her illustrations in children's books, magazine covers, and portraits of children. She was born in New York City and attended art schools in New York and Paris. She received formal recognition and awards for many of her works. In addition, she studied stained glass design at Tiffany studios.

In our collection of baby books, Clara Burd has two books: *Baby's Biography* and *Baby's Record.*

Title page illustration from *Baby's Biography*, 1913, by Clara M. Burd, published by Foster Brothers Mfg. Co. Book, $75-150.

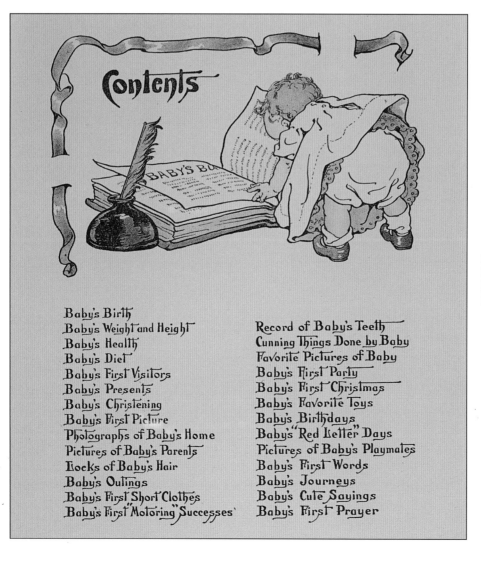

Contents

Baby's Birth
Baby's Weight and Height
Baby's Health
Baby's Diet
Baby's First Visitors
Baby's Presents
Baby's Christening
Baby's First Picture
Photographs of Baby's Home
Pictures of Baby's Parents
Locks of Baby's Hair
Baby's Outings
Baby's First Short Clothes
Baby's First "Motoring" Successes

Record of Baby's Teeth
Cunning Things Done by Baby
Favorite Pictures of Baby
Baby's First Party
Baby's First Christmas
Baby's Favorite Toys
Baby's Birthdays
Baby's "Red Letter" Days
Pictures of Baby's Playmates
Baby's First Words
Baby's Journeys
Baby's Cute Sayings
Baby's First Prayer

Illustrated contents page from *Baby's Biography*, 1913, by Clara M. Burd, published by Foster Brothers Mfg. Co.

"Photographs of Baby's Home," an illustration from *Baby's Biography*, 1913,
by Clara M. Burd, published by Foster Brothers Mfg. Co.

"Locks of Baby's Hair," an illustration from *Baby's Biography*, 1913, by
Clara M. Burd, published by Foster Brothers Mfg. Co.

"Baby's Outings," illustrated page from *Baby's Biography*, 1913, by Clara M. Burd, published by Foster Brothers Mfg. Co.

"Baby's First 'Motoring' Successes," illustrated page from *Baby's Biography*, 1913, by Clara M. Burd, published by Foster Brothers Mfg. Co.

"Cunning Things Done by Baby," illustrated page from *Baby's Biography*, 1913,
by Clara M. Burd, published by Foster Brothers Mfg. Co.

"Baby's First Christmas," an illustration from *Baby's Biography*, 1913, by Clara M. Burd, published by Foster Brothers Mfg. Co.

"Baby's First Party," illustrated page from *Baby's Biography*, 1913, by Clara M. Burd, published by Foster Brothers Mfg. Co.

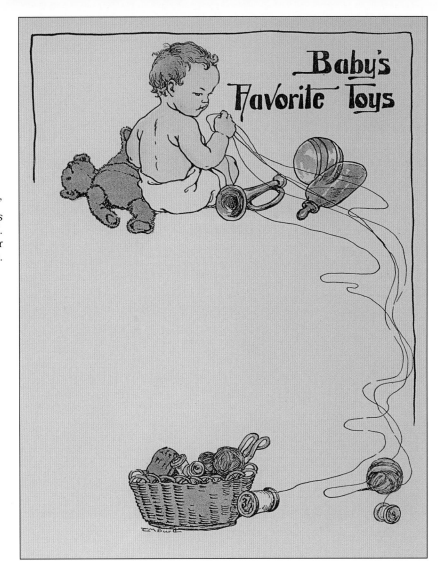

"Baby's Favorite Toys," illustrated page from *Baby's Biography*, 1913, by Clara M. Burd, published by Foster Brothers Mfg. Co.

"Baby's Birthdays," an illustration from *Baby's Biography*, 1913, by Clara M. Burd, published by Foster Brothers Mfg. Co.

"Baby's 'Red Letter' Days," illustrated page from *Baby's Biography*, 1913, by Clara M. Burd, published by Foster Brothers Mfg. Co.

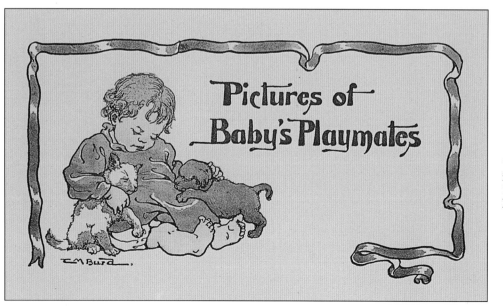

"Pictures of Baby's Playmates," an illustration from *Baby's Biography*, 1913, by Clara M. Burd, published by Foster Brothers Mfg. Co.

"Baby's First Words," illustrated page from *Baby's Biography*, 1913, by Clara M. Burd, published by Foster Brothers Mfg. Co.

"Baby's Journeys," illustrated page from *Baby's Biography*, 1913, by Clara M. Burd, published by Foster Brothers Mfg. Co.

"Baby's Cute Sayings," illustrated page from *Baby's Biography*, 1913, by Clara M. Burd, published by Foster Brothers Mfg. Co.

"Baby's First Prayer," illustrated page from *Baby's Biography*, 1913, by Clara M. Burd, published by Foster Brothers Mfg. Co.

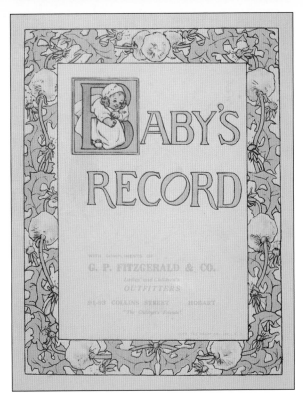

Decorated cover, *Baby's Record*, c. 1915, by Clara M. Burd, published by G. F. Fitzgerald & Co., New York. Book, $75-175.

Baby asleep, an illustration from *Baby's Record*, c. 1915, by Clara M. Burd, published by G. F. Fitzgerald & Co., New York.

Announcement of baby, an illustrated
page from *Baby's Record*, c. 1915,
by Clara M. Burd, published by G. F.
Fitzgerald & Co., New York.

"Baby's First Weight," an illustrated
page from *Baby's Record,* c. 1915, by
Clara M. Burd, published by G. F.
Fitzgerald & Co., New York.

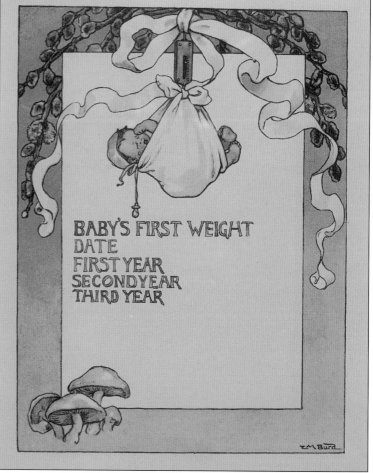

Christening page with decorations, from *Baby's Record*, c. 1915, by Clara M. Burd, published by G. F. Fitzgerald & Co., New York.

CHRISTENING

DATE

AT

BY

GIFTS

Mother and child in garden, an illustrated page from *Baby's Record*, c. 1915, by Clara M. Burd, published by G. F. Fitzgerald & Co., New York.

"Family Record," an illustrated page from *Baby's Record*, c. 1915, by Clara M. Burd, published by G. F. Fitzgerald & Co., New York.

Baby and teddy bear in tub, an illustrated page from *Baby's Record*, c. 1915, by Clara M. Burd, published by G. F. Fitzgerald & Co., New York.

"Brothers and Sisters," an illustrated page from *Baby's Record*, c. 1915, by Clara M. Burd, published by G. F. Fitzgerald & Co., New York.

Child eating in garden, an illustrated page from *Baby's Record*, c. 1915, by Clara M. Burd, published by G. F. Fitzgerald & Co., New York.

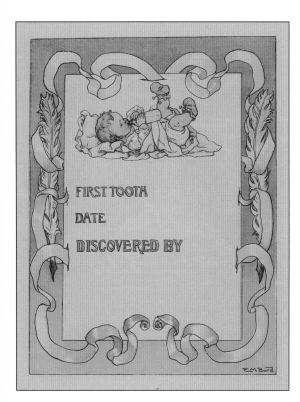

"First Tooth" page with illustration from *Baby's Record*, c. 1915, by Clara M. Burd, published by G. F. Fitzgerald & Co., New York.

Child in bed, an illustrated page from *Baby's Record*, c. 1915, by Clara M. Burd, published by G. F. Fitzgerald & Co., New York.

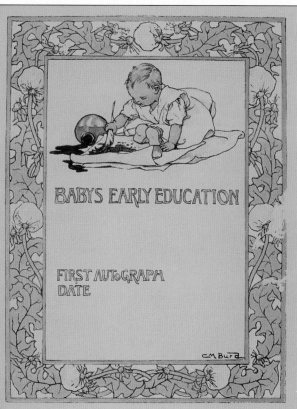

"Baby's Early Education" page from *Baby's Record*, c. 1915, by Clara M. Burd, published by G. F. Fitzgerald & Co., New York.

Child holding cat in the garden, an illustrated page from *Baby's Record*, c. 1915, by Clara M. Burd, published by G. F. Fitzgerald & Co., New York.

"Other Important Events" page from *Baby's Record*, c. 1915, by Clara M. Burd, published by G. F. Fitzgerald & Co., New York.

Bertha L. Corbett was born in 1872. She studied at the famous Howard Pyle art school in Philadelphia. The idea of the sunbonnet babies began with a group of artist friends who had gathered in her studio. As the story goes, one of the artists raised the question about how little expression there is to a figure when the face doesn't show. Miss Corbett replied that she didn't think a face was always necessary in order to make a figure expressive. She had an image in her head of a child at play with a very large sunbonnet on its head.

One of the artists challenged her reply and Miss Corbett drew her first sunbonnet baby. She made her point. Later she published a book and a primer featuring her sunbonnet babies and children. In 1910, her baby book, *Baby Days, A Sunbonnet Record,* was published.

Beautiful cloth cover with gold lettering from *Baby Days, A Sunbonnet Record,* 1910, by Bertha L. Corbett, published by Rand, McNally. Book $125-250.

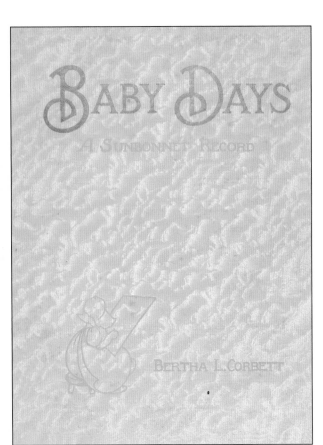

Gold fabric cover from *Baby Days, A Sunbonnet Record,* 1910, by Bertha L. Corbett, published by Rand, McNally. Book, $125-250.

Pink cover from *Baby Days, A Sunbonnet Record*, 1910, by Bertha L. Corbett, published by Rand, McNally. Book, $125-250.

Title page with lovely decorations from *Baby Days, A Sunbonnet Record*, 1910, by Bertha L. Corbett, published by Rand, McNally.

Greeting page from "The Mother of the Sunbonnet Babies" to "The Mother of the Baby who receives This Book," from *Baby Days, A Sunbonnet Record*, 1910, by Bertha L. Corbett, published by Rand, McNally.

"The Baby's Record" page from *Baby Days, A Sunbonnet Record*, 1910, by Bertha L. Corbett, published by Rand, McNally.

"Who holds the key to all hearts?" page from *Baby Days, A Sunbonnet Record*, 1910, by Bertha L. Corbett, published by Rand, McNally.

"What Color Are Its Starry Eyes?" page from *Baby Days, A Sunbonnet Record*, 1910, by Bertha L. Corbett, published by Rand, McNally.

"Place Here" page from *Baby Days, A Sunbonnet Record*, 1910, by Bertha L. Corbett, published by Rand, McNally.

"The Christening" page from *Baby Days, A Sunbonnet Record*, 1910, by Bertha L. Corbett, published by Rand, McNally.

"First Creeping" page from *Baby Days, A Sunbonnet Record*, 1910, by Bertha L. Corbett, published by Rand, McNally.

"Some Precious Pictures" page from *Baby Days, A Sunbonnet Record*, 1910, by Bertha L. Corbett, published by Rand, McNally.

"The First Tooth" page from *Baby Days, A Sunbonnet Record*, 1910, by Bertha L. Corbett, published by Rand, McNally.

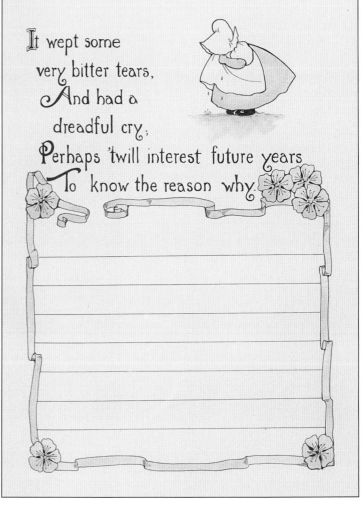

A unique illustrated page for baby's events, from *Baby Days, A Sunbonnet Record*, 1910, by Bertha L. Corbett, published by Rand, McNally.

"The First Short Dress" page from *Baby Days, A Sunbonnet Record*, 1910, by Bertha L. Corbett, published by Rand, McNally.

"What were the first wonderful words?" page from *Baby Days, A Sunbonnet Record*, 1910, by Bertha L. Corbett, published by Rand, McNally.

"The wonder-day" (when baby first walked) page from *Baby Days, A Sunbonnet Record*, 1910, by Bertha L. Corbett, published by Rand, McNally.

"What question did Baby's lips first frame?" page from *Baby Days, A Sunbonnet Record*, 1910, by Bertha L. Corbett, published by Rand, McNally.

"Note here the journeys the Baby takes" page from *Baby Days, A Sunbonnet Record*, 1910, by Bertha L. Corbett, published by Rand, McNally.

Decorated page to record events in baby's life from *Baby Days, A Sunbonnet Record*, 1910, by Bertha L. Corbett, published by Rand, McNally.

"Progressive Weight and Height" page from *Baby Days, A Sunbonnet Record*, 1910, by Bertha L. Corbett, published by Rand, McNally.

A "Baby's sayings" page from *Baby Days, A Sunbonnet Record*, 1910, by Bertha L. Corbett, published by Rand, McNally.

"The First Birthday Party" page from *Baby Days, A Sunbonnet Record*, 1910, by Bertha L. Corbett, published by Rand, McNally.

"Gifts Received" page from *Baby Days, A Sunbonnet Record*, 1910, by Bertha L. Corbett, published by Rand, McNally.

"The Darling's Dancing Lessons" page from *Baby Days, A Sunbonnet Record*, 1910, by Bertha L. Corbett, published by Rand, McNally.

"Valentines" page from *Baby Days, A Sunbonnet Record*, 1910, by Bertha L. Corbett, published by Rand, McNally.

"Childhood Friends" page from *Baby Days, A Sunbonnet Record*, 1910, by Bertha L. Corbett, published by Rand, McNally.

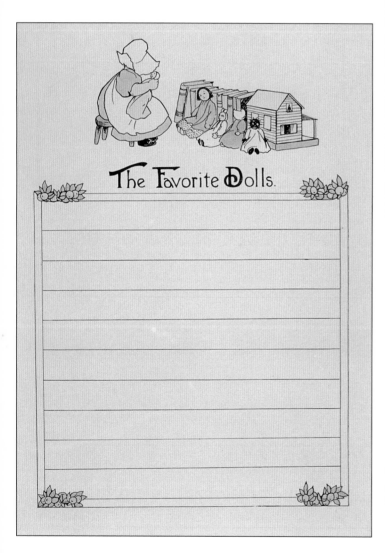

"The Favorite Dolls" page from *Baby Days, A Sunbonnet Record*, 1910, by Bertha Corbett, published by Rand, McNally.

"Favorite Books" page from *Baby Days, A Sunbonnet Record*, 1910, by Bertha L. Corbett, published by Rand, McNally.

Best loved pets page from *Baby Days, A Sunbonnet Record*, 1910, by Bertha L. Corbett, published by Rand, McNally.

"First School Day" page from *Baby Days, A Sunbonnet Record*, 1910, by Bertha L. Corbett, published by Rand, McNally.

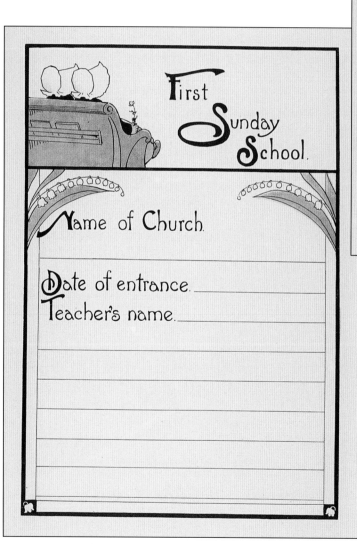

"First Sunday School" page from *Baby Days, A Sunbonnet Record*, 1910, by Bertha L. Corbett, published by Rand, McNally.

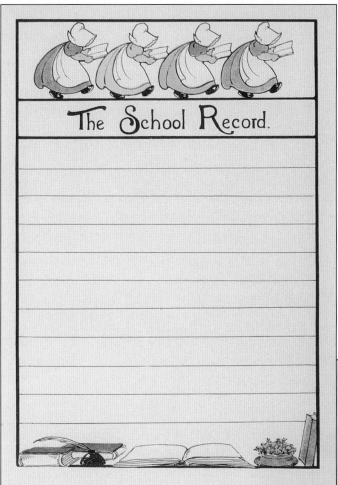

"The School Record" page from *Baby Days, A Sunbonnet Record*, 1910, by Bertha L. Corbett, published by Rand, McNally.

Baby's sweet-hearts page from *Baby Days, A Sunbonnet Record*, 1910, by Bertha L. Corbett, published by Rand, McNally.

Fanny Young Cory Cooney is better known by her professional name of Fanny Y. Cory. One of the first female comic artists in America, she grew up in the East and attended the Metropolitan School of Fine Arts in New York City in 1895. Cory married a Montana rancher and, when times got tough, renewed her wonderful artistic skills. From the 1920s to the 1950s, she was a syndicated comic strip artist. In addition she is remembered for her wonderful illustrations of various children's books. In 1907, she published her first baby book, *At the Sign of the Stork, Our Baby Book*. In 1920, her second baby book came out: *Baby Mine*.

Illustrated cover from *Baby Mine*, 1920, by Fanny Y. Cory, published by Brown & Bigelow, Minneapolis. Book, $125-250.

"Record of Birth," illustrated page from *Baby Mine*, 1920, by Fanny Y. Cory, published by Brown & Bigelow, Minneapolis.

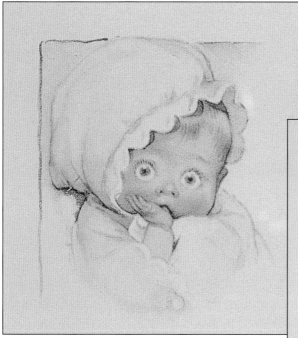

Baby with bonnet sucking its thumb, illustration from *Baby Mine*, 1920, by Fanny Y. Cory, published by Brown & Bigelow, Minneapolis.

"Oh here I am…," illustrated page with poem from *Baby Mine,* 1920, by Fanny Y. Cory, published by Brown & Bigelow, Minneapolis.

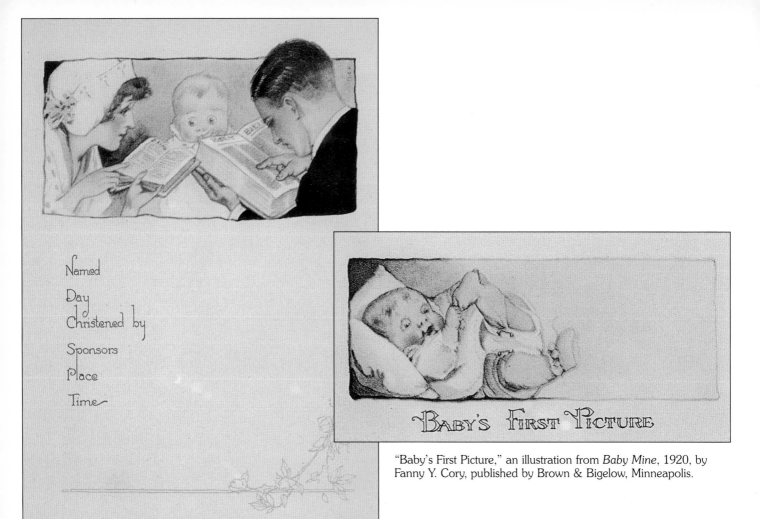

Named

Day

Christened by

Sponsors

Place

Time

Christening page from *Baby Mine*, 1920, by Fanny Y. Cory,
published by Brown & Bigelow, Minneapolis.

"Baby's First Picture," an illustration from *Baby Mine*, 1920, by
Fanny Y. Cory, published by Brown & Bigelow, Minneapolis.

"Baby's First Presents," illustrated page from *Baby Mine*, 1920, by
Fanny Y. Cory, published by Brown & Bigelow, Minneapolis.

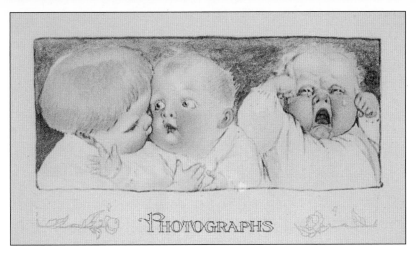

"Photographs" page illustration from *Baby Mine*, 1920, by Fanny Y. Cory, published by Brown & Bigelow, Minneapolis.

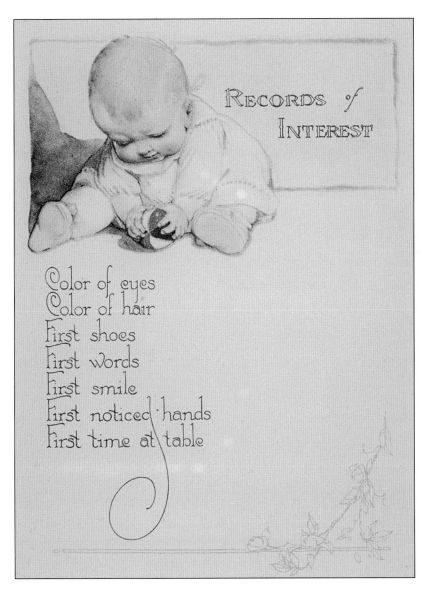

"Records of Interest," illustrated page from *Baby Mine*, 1920, by Fanny Y. Cory, published by Brown & Bigelow, Minneapolis.

The
FIRST TIME

First short clothes
First visitors
First ride
First crept
First stood alone
First walked

"The First Time," illustrated page from *Baby Mine*, 1920, by Fanny Y. Cory, published by Brown & Bigelow, Minneapolis.

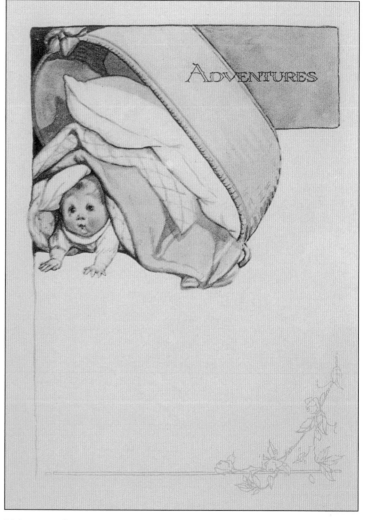

ADVENTURES

"Adventures" page with charming illustration from *Baby Mine*, 1920, by Fanny Y. Cory, published by Brown & Bigelow, Minneapolis.

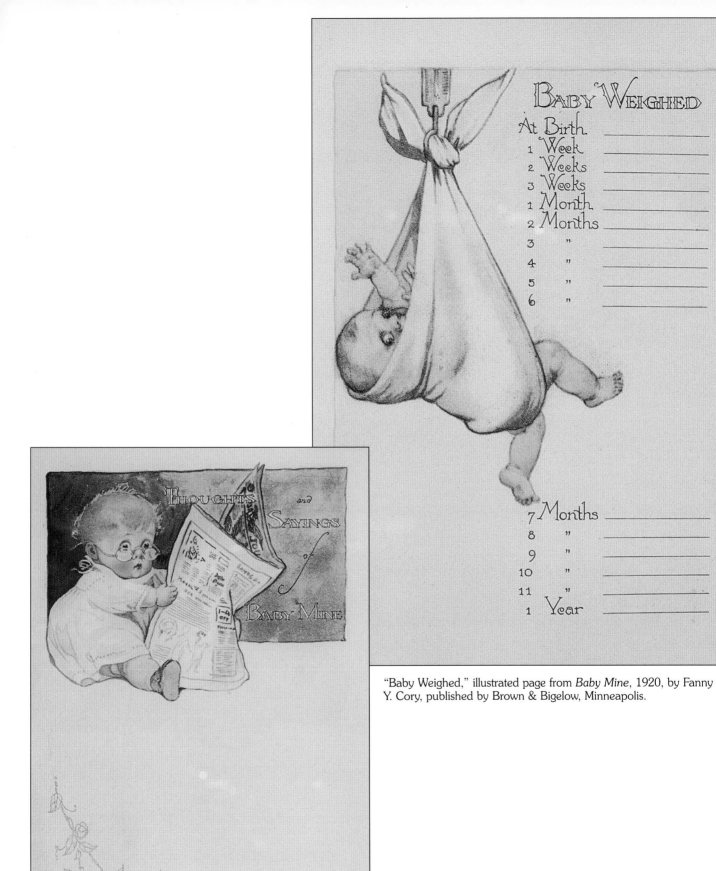

"Baby Weighed," illustrated page from *Baby Mine*, 1920, by Fanny Y. Cory, published by Brown & Bigelow, Minneapolis.

"Thoughts and Sayings" page with delightful illustration from *Baby Mine*, 1920, by Fanny Y. Cory, published by Brown & Bigelow, Minneapolis.

"The First Birthday," illustrated page from
Baby Mine, 1920, by Fanny Y. Cory, published
by Brown & Bigelow, Minneapolis.

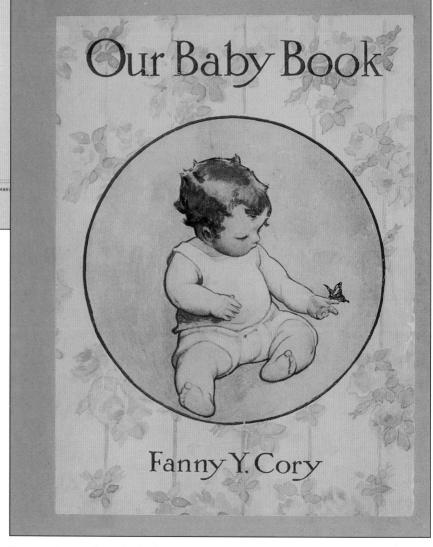

Decorated cover from *At the Sign of the Stork: Our Baby Book,* 1907, by
Fanny Y. Cory, published by Bobbs-Merrill Co., Indianapolis. Book, $100-250.

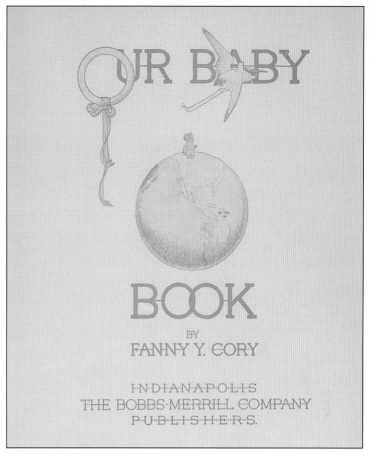

Decorated title page from *At the Sign of the Stork: Our Baby Book*, 1907, by Fanny Y. Cory, published by Bobbs-Merrill Co., Indianapolis.

Frontispiece from *At the Sign of the Stork: Our Baby Book*, 1907, by Fanny Y. Cory, published by Bobbs-Merrill Co., Indianapolis.

"The Arrival," illustrated page with verse from *At the Sign of the Stork: Our Baby Book*, by Fanny Y. Cory, published by Bobbs-Merrill Co., Indianapolis.

HERE I stand, alone and shy,
A baby unadorned;
Some mother-heart must surely spy
An object of such sympathy,
Or else I'm misinformed.

THE ARRIVAL

Melcena Burns Denny was a California researcher, dramatist, author, and artist. She was born near Auburn, California and taught school in Scott Valley. She wrote many magazine articles and several books, including an illustrated book of poems for children and other poems. In 1905, she did a baby book called *The Book of Baby Mine.*

Soft leather cover, *The Book of Baby Mine,* 1915, by Melcena Burns Denny, published by The Simplicity Company, Grand Rapids. Book, $50-150.

Baby's name page, with delightful decorations and verse from
The Book of Baby Mine, 1915, by Melcena Burns Denny,
published by The Simplicity Company, Grand Rapids.

Title page with lovely decorations from
The Book of Baby Mine, 1915, by
Melcena Burns Denny, published by The
Simplicity Company, Grand Rapids.

This page has a place for the doctor and nurse to sign and a space for a photo of the baby's first home, from *The Book of Baby Mine*, 1915, by Melcena Burns Denny, published by The Simplicity Company, Grand Rapids.

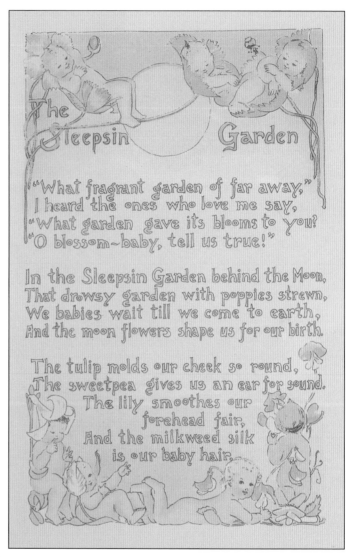

"The Sleepin Garden" page with verse and lovely decorations from *The Book of Baby Mine*, 1915, by Melcena Burns Denny, published by The Simplicity Company, Grand Rapids.

"Mother's Family Tree," an illustrated page from *The Book of Baby Mine*, 1915, by Melcena Burns Denny, published by The Simplicity Company, Grand Rapids.

"Father's Family Tree," an illustrated page from *The Book of Baby Mine*, 1915, by Melcena Burns Denny, published by The Simplicity Company, Grand Rapids.

My First Prayer

I learned this when I was _____ old.

Now I lay me down to sleep,
I pray the Lord my soul to keep.
God bless my mother and father dear,
And, Heavenly Father, draw me near,
And bless me now, and let me wake,
A good little child, for Jesus' sake.
~Amen.

Other Forget~me~nots.

"My First Prayer" page with lovely decoration and verse from *The Book of Baby Mine*,
by Melcena Burns Denny, published by The Simplicity Company, Grand Rapids.

Decorated cover from *The Flower Song,* 1930, by Carlyle Emery,
published by Von Hoffman Press, St. Louis. Book, $75-150.

Title page illustration from *The Flower Song,* 1930, by Carlyle Emery, published by Von Hoffman Press, St. Louis.

"To my Child" page from *The Flower Song*, 1930, by Carlyle Emery, published by Von Hoffman Press, St. Louis.

To my Child

WHEN Mother and Daddy were little children - just your age - they wanted to know the same things that you want to know now. They, too, wanted to know the answer to the big question that has been in your mind for some time.

The answer is as beautiful as Life itself and you will find it in the Flower Song.

Read this little story - not just once, but over and over again. Then ask questions if you do not understand all of it.

And always remember, dear, God gives us the answer to all questions and His great wisdom is infinite and everlasting.

Full page illustration from *The Flower Song*, 1930, by Carlyle
Emery, published by Von Hoffman Press, St. Louis.

Illustrated cover from *Baby's Own Book,* 1923, by N. Farini. Book, $50-150.

Decorated title page from *Baby's Own Book,* 1923, by N. Farini.

"Greetings" page from *Baby's Own Book,* 1923, by N. Farini.

Pink cloth cover from *Baby*, (1915) 1921, by Meta Morris Grimball, published by Cupples & Leon Co., New York. Book, $100-200.

Child with bouquet of roses, illustration from *Baby*, (1915) 1921, by Meta Morris Grimball, published by Cupples & Leon Co., New York.

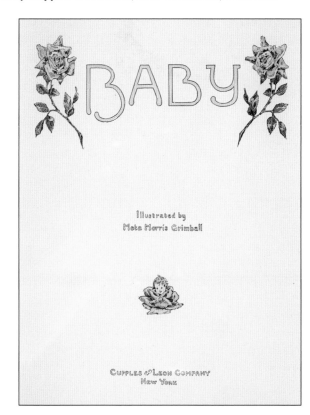

Decorated title Page from *Baby*, (1915) 1921, by Meta Morris Grimball, published by Cupples & Leon Co., New York.

Lovely decorated "Baby Is Born" page from *Baby*, (1915) 1921,by Meta Morris Grimball, published by Cupples & Leon Co., New York.

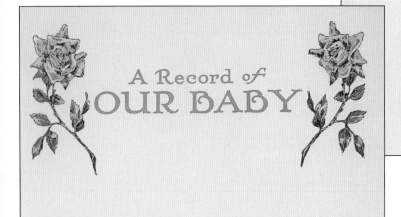

Decorated title page from *A Record of Our Baby*, 1921, by Meta Morris Grimball, published by Cupples & Leon Co., New York. Book, $125-200.

Born in 1876, Bessie Pease Gutmann grew up in Philadelphia and attended the Philadelphia School of Design for Women. She continued her art education at the New York School of Art and the Art Students League of New York.

She had already begun her art career when she married Hellmuth Gutmann, a printer, thus combining their talents and building a very successful book and publishing business.

Her artistic ability was exceptional. Gutmann's babies and children are memorable with an inherent warmth about each one. Her baby books were *The Biography of Our Baby,* 1906, and *Our Baby's Early Days,* 1908, the latter in collaboration with Meta Morris Grimball.

Blue cover with gold lettering from *The Biography of Our Baby,* 1906, by Edmund Vance Cooke and illustrated by Bessie Collins Pease Gutmann, published by Dodge Publishing Company, New York. Book, $125-250.

The Biography Of Our Baby

With Drawings by Bessie Collins Pease

THE FIRST LESSON

Frontispiece, "The First Lesson," from *The Biography of Our Baby*, 1906, by Edmund Vance Cooke and illustrated by Bessie Collins Pease Gutmann. Published by Dodge Publishing Company, New York.

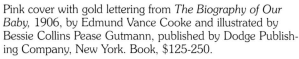

Pink cover with gold lettering from *The Biography of Our Baby*, 1906, by Edmund Vance Cooke and illustrated by Bessie Collins Pease Gutmann, published by Dodge Publishing Company, New York. Book, $125-250.

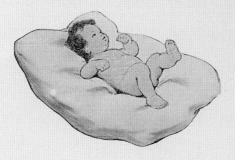

THE BIOGRAPHY
OF OUR BABY

Verses by

EDMUND VANCE COOKE

Author of " Chronicles of the Little Tot "
" Rimes to Be Read," etc.

with Drawings by

BESSIE COLLINS PEASE

New York

DODGE PUBLISHING COMPANY

33d St. Eighth Avenue 34th St.

Decorated title page from *The Biography of Our Baby,* 1906, by Edmund Vance Cooke and illustrated by Bessie Collins Pease Gutmann, published by Dodge Publishing Company, New York.

Mother and baby, an illustrated page from *The Biography of Our Baby,* 1906, by Edmund Vance Cooke and illustrated by Bessie Collins Pease Gutmann, published by Dodge Publishing Company, New York.

OUR BABY'S PLAYMATES

"Our Baby's Playmates," illustration from *The Biography of Our Baby*, 1906, by Edmund Vance Cooke and illustrated by Bessie Collins Pease Gutmann, published by Dodge Publishing Company, New York.

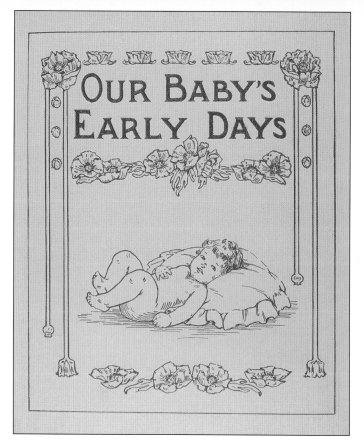

Blue cover from *Our Baby's Early Days*, 1908, by Bessie Pease Gutmann and Meta Morris Grimball. published by Best & Co., New York. Book, $200-400.

Baby on pillow, beautiful illustration from *Our Baby's Early Days*, 1908, by Bessie Pease Gutmann and Meta Morris Grimball, published by Best & Company, New York.

Mother and baby, an illustrated page from *Our Baby's Early Days*, 1908, by Bessie Pease Gutmann and Meta Morris Grimball, published by Best & Co., New York.

"Baby Has an Outing Page" from *Our Baby's Early Days*, 1908, by Bessie Pease Gutmann and Meta Morris Grimball, published by Best & Co., New York.

"Baby Tries To Walk," illustrated page from *Our Baby's Early Days*, 1908, by Bessie Pease Gutmann and Meta Morris Grimball, published by Best & Co., New York.

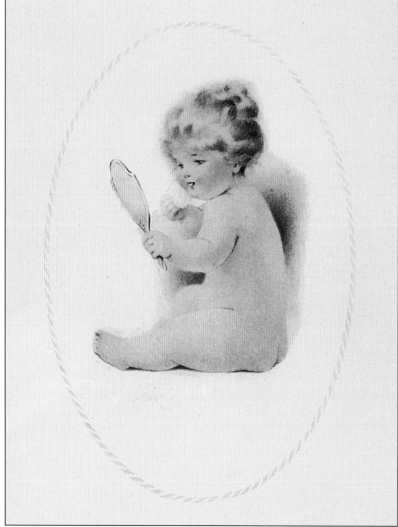

Baby looking in mirror, illustration from *Our Baby's Early Days*, 1908, by Bessie Pease Gutmann and Meta Morris Grimball, published by Best & Co., New York.

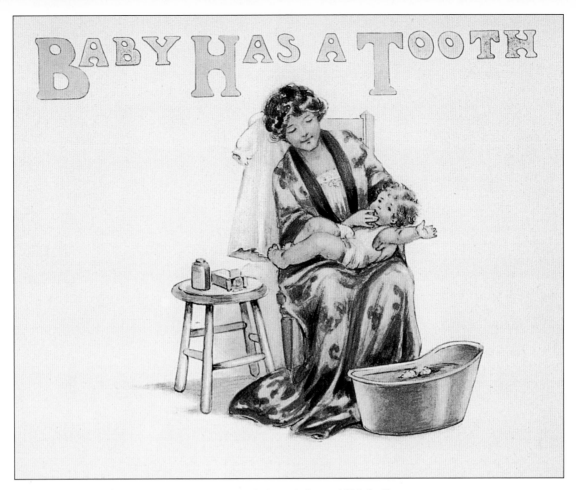

"Baby Has a Tooth," an illustration from *Our Baby's Early Days*, 1908, by Bessie Pease Gutmann and Meta Morris Grimball, published by Best & Co., New York.

Baby and butterfly, lovely illustration from *Our Baby's Early Days*, 1908, by Bessie Pease Gutmann and Meta Morris Grimball, published by Best & Company, New York.

Mother and baby, illustrated page from *Our Baby's Early Days*, 1908, by Bessie Pease
Gutmann and Meta Morris Grimball, published by Best & Co., New York.

The Illustrators of Baby Books: Bessie Pease Gutmann

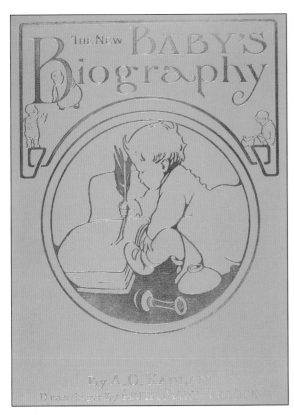

Pink embossed cover, *The New Baby's Biography*, (1891) 1908, by A. O. Kaplan and illustrated by Ruth Mary Hallock, published by Brentano's, New York. Book, $200-400.

Decorated title page from *The New Baby's Biography*, (1891) 1908, by A. O. Kaplan and illustrated by Ruth Mary Hallock, published by Brentano's, New York.

"Baby's Friends," illustration from *The New Baby's Biography*, (1891) 1908, by A. O. Kaplan and illustrated by Ruth Mary Hallock, published by Brentano's, New York.

"Welcome Little Stranger," an illustrated page from *The New Baby's Biography*, (1891) 1908, by A. O. Kaplan and illustrated by Ruth Mary Hallock, published by Brentano's, New York.

"Baby was Weighed," an illustrated page with verse from *The New Baby's Biography*, (1891) 1908, by A. O. Kaplan and illustrated by Ruth Mary Hallock, published by Brentano's, New York.

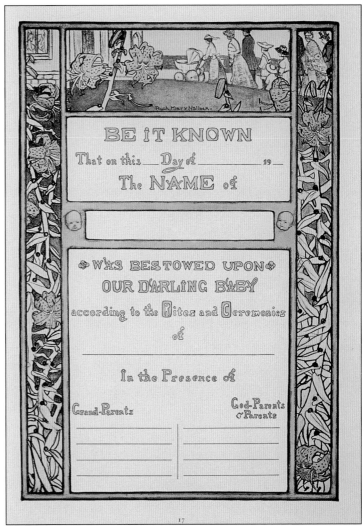

Baby's name page with lovely decorations from *The New Baby's Biography*, (1891) 1908, by A. O. Kaplan and illustrated by Ruth Mary Hallock, published by Brentano's, New York.

"Our Baby Pealed Forth Its First Laugh," illustrated page from *The New Baby's Biography*, (1891) 1908, by A. O. Kaplan and illustrated by Ruth Mary Hallock, published by Brentano's, New York.

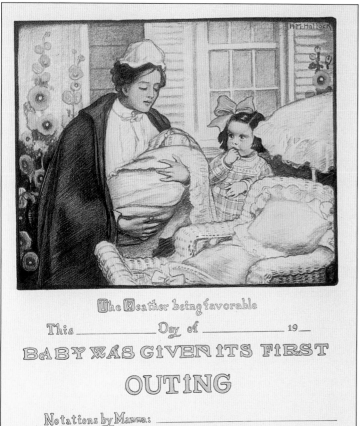

"Baby Was Given Its First Outing," illustrated page from *The New Baby's Biography*, (1891) 1908, by A. O. Kaplan and illustrated by Ruth Mary Hallock, published by Brentano's, New York.

First haircut page with verse from *The New Baby's Biography*, (1891) 1908, by A. O. Kaplan and illustrated by Ruth Mary Hallock, published by Brentano's, New York.

"Baby's First Shoes," illustrated page from *The New Baby's Biography*, (1891) 1908, by A. O. Kaplan and illustrated by Ruth Mary Hallock, published by Brentano's, New York.

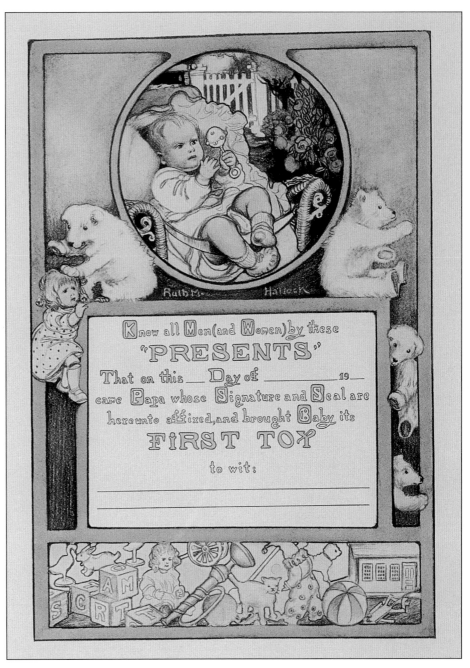

"First Toy," illustrated page from *The New Baby's Biography*, (1891) 1908, by A. O. Kaplan and illustrated by Ruth Mary Hallock, published by Brentano's, New York.

"Baby Spoke Its First Word," illustrated page from *The New Baby's Biography*. (1891) 1908, by A. O. Kaplan and illustrated by Ruth Mary Hallock, published by Brentano's, New York.

"Short Skirt," illustrated page from *The New Baby's Biography*, (1891) 1908, by A. O. Kaplan and illustrated by Ruth Mary Hallock, published by Brentano's, New York.

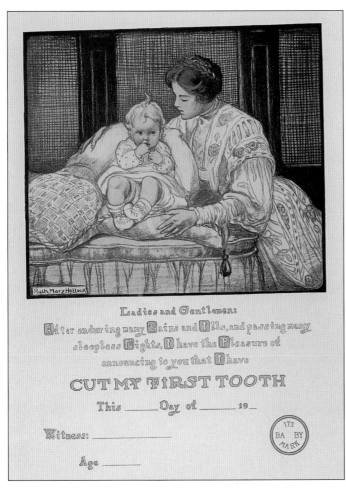

"Cut My First Tooth," illustrated page from *The New Baby's Biography*, (1891) 1908, by A. O. Kaplan and illustrated by Ruth Mary Hallock, published by Brentano's, New York.

"The First Birthday Party," illustrated page from *The New Baby's Biography*, (1891) 1908, by A. O. Kaplan and illustrated by Ruth Mary Hallock, published by Brentano's, New York.

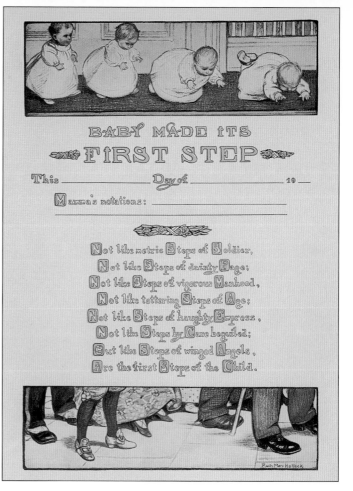

"Baby Made Its First Step," illustrated page with verse from *The New Baby's Biography*, (1891) 1908, by A. O. Kaplan and illustrated by Ruth Mary Hallock, published by Brentano's, New York.

"Our Infant Started Creeping," illustrated page from *The New Baby's Biography*, (1891) 1908, by A. O. Kaplan and illustrated by Ruth Mary Hallock, published by Brentano's, New York.

"A Merry Christmas Eve," illustrated page from *The New Baby's Biography*, (1891) 1908, by A. O. Kaplan and illustrated by Ruth Mary Hallock, published by Brentano's, New York.

"First Time at a Place of Public Worship," illustrated page from *The New Baby's Biography*, (1891) 1908, by A. O. Kaplan and illustrated by Ruth Mary Hallock, published by Brentano's, New York.

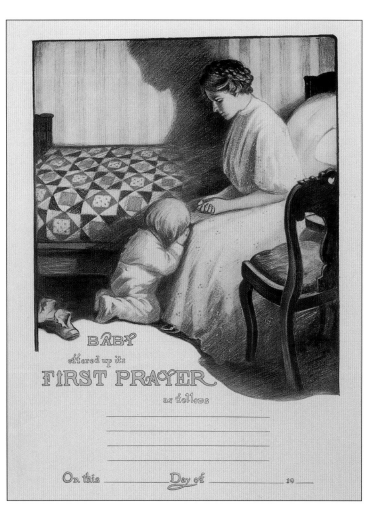

"First Prayer," illustrated page from *The New Baby's Biography*, (1891) 1908, by A. O. Kaplan and illustrated by Ruth Mary Hallock, published by Brentano's, New York.

"Dancing Lessons," illustrated page from *The New Baby's Biography*, (1891) 1908, by A. O. Kaplan and illustrated by Ruth Mary Hallock, published by Brentano's, New York.

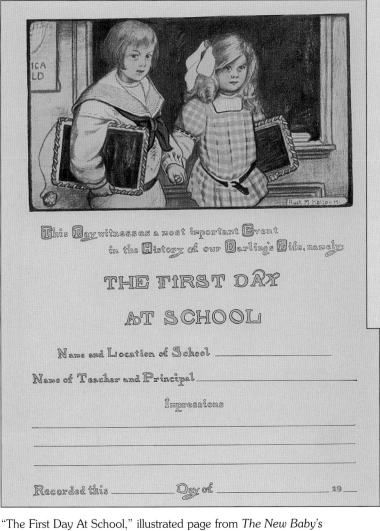

"The First Day At School," illustrated page from *The New Baby's Biography*, (1891) 1908, by A. O. Kaplan and illustrated by Ruth Mary Hallock, published by Brentano's, New York.

Queen Holden is one of the best known paper doll artists. She started drawing paper dolls for Whitman Publishers in 1929 and continued to work for them for the next twenty years. Her "Glamour Dolls" of the 1941-1942 period were the inspiration for the now famous "Barbie Doll." Her baby illustrations are winsome and very dear pictures.

Holden's two baby books are *Baby Mine, Baby's Book of Events*, c. 1920, and *Our Baby*, 1927.

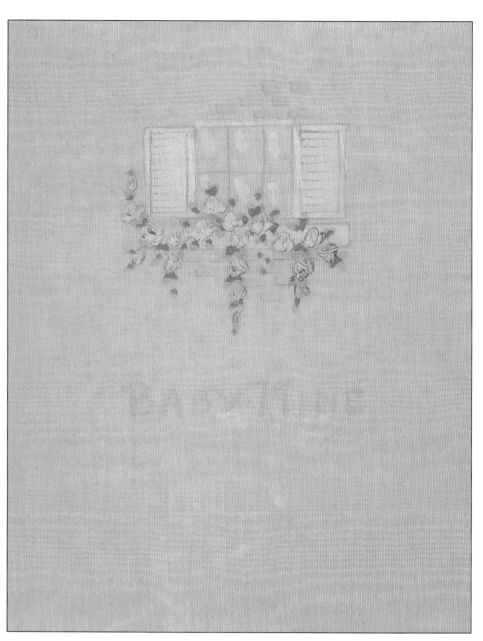

Illustrated cloth cover from *Baby Mine, Baby's Book of Events*, c. 1920, by Queen Holden, published by Richard G. Krueger Inc., New York. Book, $75-150.

Title page from *Baby Mine, Baby's Book of Events*, c. 1920, by Queen Holden, published by Richard G. Krueger Inc., New York.

"Baby Arrived," illustrated page from *Baby Mine, Baby's Book of Events*, c. 1920, by Queen Holden, published by Richard G. Krueger, Inc., New York.

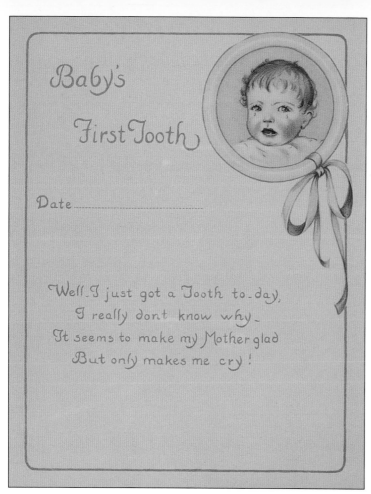

"Baby's First Tooth," illustrated page with verse from *Baby Mine, Baby's Book of Events*, c. 1920, by Queen Holden, published by Richard G. Krueger, Inc., New York.

"Our Baby's First Word," illustrated page from *Baby Mine, Baby's Book of Events*, c. 1920, by Queen Holden, published by Richard G. Krueger, Inc., New York

"First Christmas," illustrated page (a rare illustration of Santa Claus in a baby book) from *Baby Mine, Baby's Book of Events*, c. 1920, by Queen Holden, published by Richard G. Krueger, Inc., New York.

"Baby's Little Playmates," illustrated page from *Baby Mine, Baby's Book of Events* c. 1920, by Queen Holden, published by Richard G. Krueger, Inc., New York.

Blue cover from *Our Baby,* 1927, by
Queen Holden, published by Richard G.
Krueger Inc., New York. Book, $75-150.

On................19.....our little Baby came.
.........................we chose to be h.....name.
They knew we wanted h.....I guess,
'Cause.........................was the address.

Mother ------------------------
Father -----------------------
Doctor ----------------------
Nurse ----------------------

TIME

"Little Baby Came," illustrated page from *Our
Baby,* 1927, by Queen Holden, published by
Richard G. Krueger, Inc., New York.

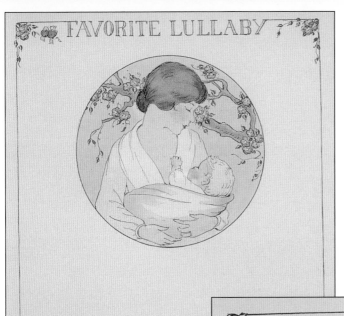

"Favorite Lullaby," illustrated page from *Our Baby*. 1927, by Queen Holden, published by Richard G. Krueger, Inc., New York.

"Baby's First Outing," illustrated page from *Our Baby*, 1927, by Queen Holden, published by Richard G. Krueger, Inc., New York.

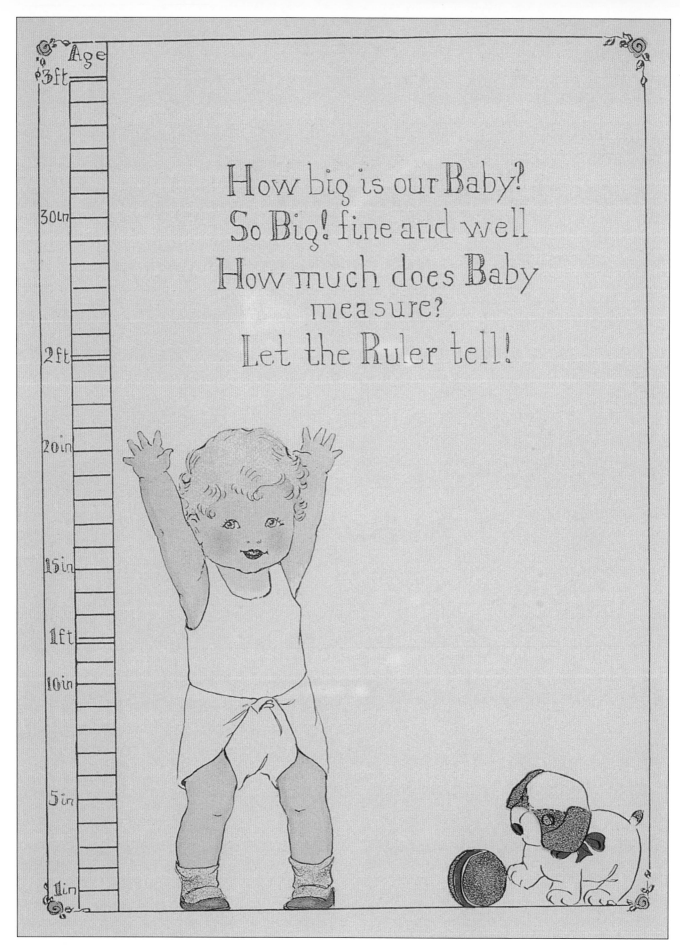

How big is our Baby?
So Big! fine and well
How much does Baby measure?
Let the Ruler tell!

"How big is our Baby," illustrated page from *Our Baby*, 1927, by Queen Holden, published by Richard G. Krueger Inc., New York.

"First little new Shoes," illustrated page from *Our Baby*, 1927, by Queen Holden, published by Richard G. Krueger Inc., New York.

"The First few Steps our Baby took," illustrated page from *Our Baby*, 1927, by Queen Holden, published by Richard G. Krueger, Inc., New York.

Baby's hair page, with a lock of hair, from *Our Baby*, 1927, by
Queen Holden, published by Richard G. Krueger, Inc., New York.

"Baby's First Party," illustrated page from *Our Baby*, 1927, by
Queen Holden, published by Richard G. Krueger, Inc., New York.

Maud Humphrey was famous for her paintings of nursery children costumed in elaborate hats and dresses. It is reported that she used her young son, Humphrey Bogart, as a model, posing him in both boy and girl outfits. In 1898, she married Dr. Belmont De Forest Bogart.

At the beginning of the twentieth century, she had become one the highest paid and most popular artists in America. She received worldwide recognition for her drawings and illustrations, which appeared in books, on postcards, as calendars, and in commercial advertisements and popular magazines of the day.

Humphrey did one baby book, *Baby Records,* which was published in 1898 and printed for many years thereafter. This baby book was available with a choice of one color illustration, six color illustrations, or twelve color illustrations, as well as different covers.

Paisley print cloth cover of *Baby's Record,* 1898, by Maud Humphrey, published by Frederick A. Stokes Co., New York. Book, $300-500.

Blue cover with silver lettering, *Baby's Record*, 1898, by Maud Humphrey, published by Frederick A. Stokes Co., New York. Book, $300-500.

Title page (stating that this edition has twelve color illustrations) from *Baby's Record*, 1898, by Maud Humphrey, published by Frederick A. Stokes Co., New York.

Frontispiece, baby with bouquet of pink roses and petals, from *Baby's Record*, 1898, by Maud Humphrey, published by Frederick A. Stokes Co., New York.

Baby in carriage with sister looking on, an illustrated page from *Baby's Record*, 1898, by Maud Humphrey, published by Frederick A. Stokes Co., New York.

Mother, child and sister, an illustrated page from *Baby's Record*, 1898, by Maud Humphrey, published by Frederick A. Stokes Co., New York.

Christmas time and child with an ornament, an illustrated page from *Baby's Record,* 1898, by Maud Humphrey, published by Frederick A. Stokes Co., New York.

Child taking first steps, an illustrated page from *Baby's Record,* 1898, by Maud Humphrey, published by Frederick A. Stokes Co., New York.

First birthday, an illustrated page from *Baby's Record*, 1898, by
Maud Humphrey, published by Frederick A. Stokes Co., New York.

COPYRIGHT 1898 BY FREDERICK A. STOKES COMPANY.
PRINTED IN AMERICA.

Mother and child in prayer, an illustrated page from *Baby's Record*, 1898,
by Maud Humphrey, published by Frederick A. Stokes Co., New York.

Child opening valentine, an illustrated page from
Baby's Record, 1898, by Maud Humphrey,
published by Frederick A. Stokes Co., New York.

Child in garden gathering flowers, an
illustration from *Baby's Record*, 1898, by
Maud Humphrey, published by Frederick
A. Stokes Co., New York.

Child wearing lovely hat with chalkboard, an illustration from
Baby's Record, 1898, by Maud Humphrey, published by Frederick
A. Stokes Co., New York.

Child sitting in church, an illustrated page from *Baby's
Record*, 1898, by Maud Humphrey, published by
Frederick A. Stokes Co., New York.

Child in lovely pink dress, an illustration from *Baby's Record*, 1898, by
Maud Humphrey, published by Frederick A. Stokes Co., New York.

Henrietta Willebeek Le Mair was the daughter of a wealthy corn merchant in Rotterdam. Her parents were both artists who wrote verses for their daughter to illustrate during her youth. In France, she published her first book at the age of fifteen. In 1911, she created a series of nursery rhyme illustrations for the music publisher, Augener in London and McKay in America.

Her one baby book is *Baby's Diary*, c. 1890.

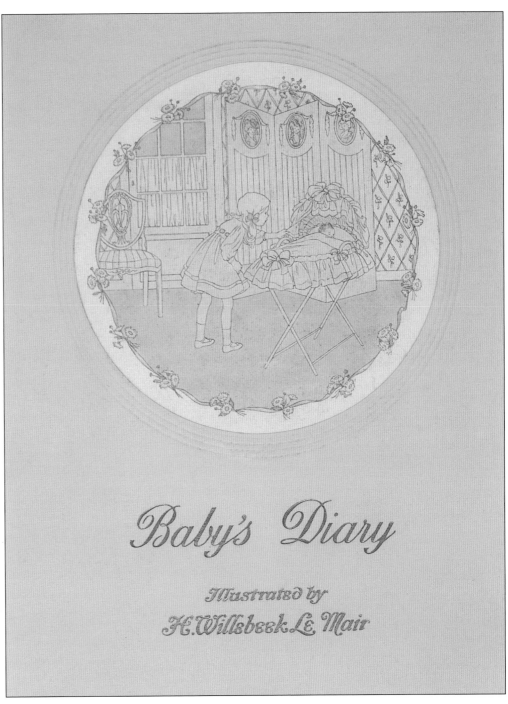

Decorated cover from *Baby's Diary*, 1890, by H. Willebeek Le Mair, published by Augener, Ltd., London. Book, $200-450.

Sister and baby, an illustration from *Baby's Diary*, 1890, by H. Willebeeck Le Mair, published by Augener, Ltd., London.

Toddler with children, an illustration from *Baby's Diary*, 1890, H. Willebeeck Le Mair, published by Augener, Ltd., London.

Baby in carriage for walk, an illustration from *Baby's Diary*. 1890, by H. Willebeeck Le Mair, published by Augener, Ltd., London.

Baby in long gown with nurse, an illustration
from *Baby's Diary,* 1890, by H. Willebeeck Le
Mair, published by Augener, Ltd., London.

Pink cover from *Babyhood Days*, 1915, by Jessie Alma Pierson,
published by Barse & Hopkins, New York. Book, $75-150.

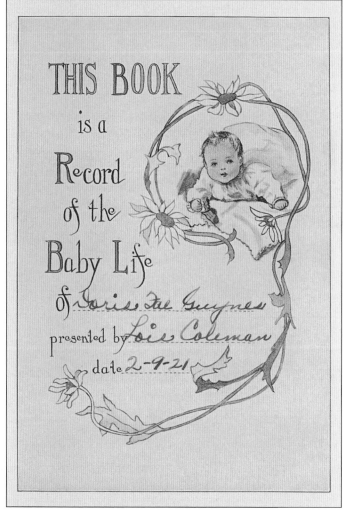

"This Book is a Record," an illustrated page from
Babyhood Days, 1915, by Jessie Alma Pierson,
published by Barse & Hopkins, New York.

Mother and baby illustration from *Baby-hood Days*, 1915, by Jessie Alma Pierson, published by Barse & Hopkins, New York.

Title page from *Babyhood Days*, 1915, by Jessie Alma Pierson, published by Barse & Hopkins, New York.

Babyhood Days
decorated by
Jessie Alma Pierson
frontispiece by
Evelyn von Hartmann

New York
Barse & Hopkins
Publishers.

Frontispiece from *Baby's History,* (1890) 1900, by S. D. Runyan, published by Frederick A. Stokes Co., New York.

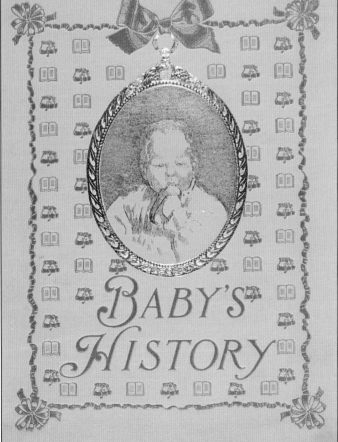

Blue cover from *Baby's History,* (1890) 1900, by S. D. Runyan, published by Frederick A. Stokes Co., New York. Book, $100-250.

Baby and sister, an
illustration from *Baby's
History,* (1890) 1900, by
S. D. Runyan, published
by Frederick A. Stokes
Co., New York.

First birthday, an illustrated page from *Baby's History*, (1890) 1900, by S. D. Runyan, published by Frederick A. Stokes Co., New York.

Children feeding chicken and chicks, an illustration from *Baby's History*, (1890)
1900, by S. D. Runyan, published by Frederick A. Stokes Co., New York.

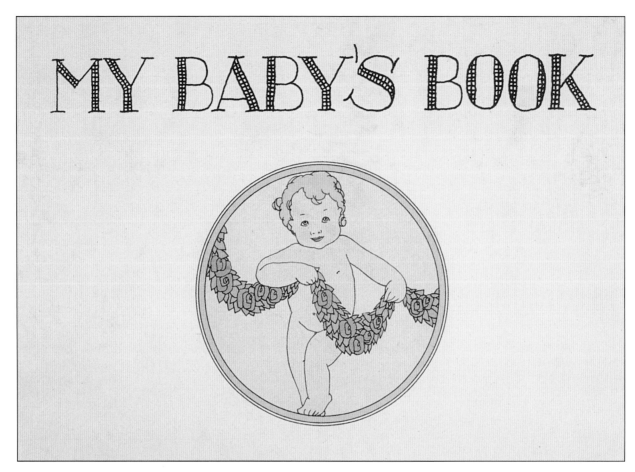

Decorated cover from *My Baby's Book*, 1927, by E. Schacherer, published by Laird & Lee, Chicago. Book, $75-150.

Decorated end pages from *My Baby's Book*, 1927, by E. Schacherer, published by Laird & Lee, Chicago.

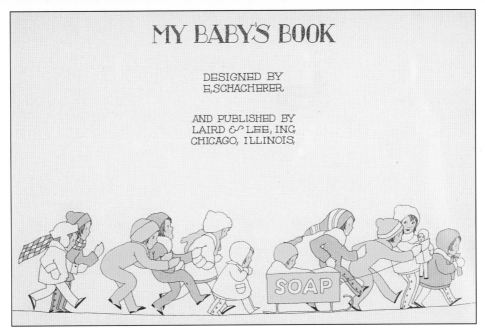

Title page from *My Baby's Book*, 1927, by E. Schacherer, published by Laird & Lee, Chicago.

Announcement page with decorations from *My Baby's Book*, 1927 by E. Schacherer, published by Laird & Lee, Chicago.

BABY

DID you ever look over
The side of a crib
And see two little eyes of blue?
And two little hands,
So chubby and white,
That wriggle and reach for you?
Two cute little ears,
So tiny a nose,
And a mouth puckered up to say "Goo"?
What is more precious
In all this wide world
Than a baby—unless it is two?

—G. A. R.

From "The Line," Chicago Tribune.

Baby poem with wonderful decorations from *My Baby's Book*, 1927, by E. Schacherer, published by Laird & Lee, Chicago.

Jessie Wilcox Smith was the pre-eminent student from among Howard Pyle's students. She was a very popular and well known artist in America from 1900 to 1930. She did wonderful drawings and lush oil paintings of her subjects. She specialized in children and stories for children. In addition to her illustrations for many books, her work often appeared in *Good Housekeeping* and *McClures,* both very popular magazines of the time.

Smith's one baby book was *Baby's Red Letter Days,* issued in 1901 and again in 1906, which came in several different covers.

Decorated cover from *Baby's Red Letter Days,* 1901, by Jessie Wilcox Smith, published by Just Foods, Syracuse. Book, $125-250.

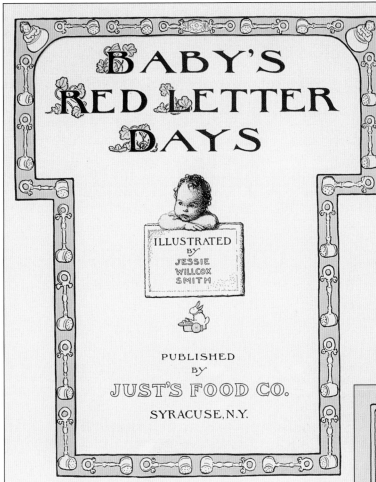

Title page with decorations from
Baby's Red Letter Days, 1901,
by Jessie Wilcox Smith, published by Just Foods, Syracuse.

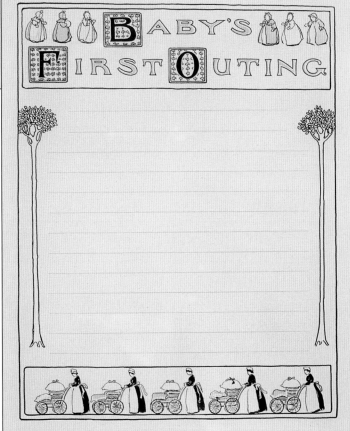

"Baby's First Outing," illustrated page from
Baby's Red Letter Days, 1901, by Jessie Wilcox
Smith, published by Just Foods, Syracuse.

Stork with baby, an illustrated page from *Baby's Red Letter Days*,
1901, by Jessie Wilcox Smith, published by Just Foods, Syracuse.

Mother holding baby, an illustrated page from *Baby's Red Letter Days*,
1901, by Jessie Wilcox Smith, published by Just Foods, Syracuse.

Father, mother and child, an illustrated page from *Baby's Red Letter Days*,
1901, by Jessie Wilcox Smith. Published by Just Foods, Syracuse.

The first step, an illustrated page from *Baby's Red Letter Days*,
1901, by Jessie Wilcox Smith, published by Just Foods, Syracuse.

Ida Waugh was the daughter of painter Samuel B. Waugh of Philadelphia. She began her studies at the Philadelphia Academy of Fine Art. Her work was exhibited at the Paris Salons of 1889, 1890, and 1891. In 1896, she won the Norman W. Dodge Prize at the National Academy of Design in New York City.

Waugh did illustrations for children's books and magazines, with her lifelong companion Amy Blanchard who owned a neighboring summer cottage in Maine.

Her baby book was *Baby Days*, 1880, with Amy Neally as author. In addition, we have identified her as the unstated illustrator of two baby books in our collection: *My Baby's Biography* and *Record of Our Baby*.

Blue cover from *Baby Days*, 1880, by Amy Neally with illustrations by Ida Waugh, Eddie J. Andrews, and Harriett M. Bennett, published by E. P. Dutton & Co., New York. Book, $100-250.

Mother and baby illustration from *Baby Days*, 1880, by Amy Neally with illustrations by Ida Waugh, Eddie J. Andrews, and Harriett M. Bennett, published by E. P. Dutton & Co., New York.

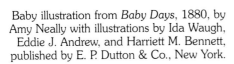

Baby illustration from *Baby Days*, 1880, by Amy Neally with illustrations by Ida Waugh, Eddie J. Andrew, and Harriett M. Bennett, published by E. P. Dutton & Co., New York.

LEARNING TO CREEP.

This is the Baby I love!
    The Baby that cannot talk;
    The Baby that cannot walk;
The Baby that just begins to creep;
The Baby that's cuddled
          and rocked to sleep;
    Oh! this is the Baby I love.

"Learning To Creep," illustrated page with verse from *Baby Days*, 1880, by Amy Neally with illustrations by Ida Waugh, Eddie J. Andrew, and Harriett M. Bennett, published by E. P. Dutton & Co., New York.

Mother and baby illustration from *Baby Days*, 1880, by Amy Neally with illustrations by Ida Waugh, Eddie J. Andrew, and Harriett M. Bennett, published by E. P. Dutton & Co., New York.

BABY IN THE COUNTRY

My Aunty has written
to Mamma,
And says that she wants
me to come
And stay through the long,
hot summer
In her beautiful
country
home.

"Baby in the Country," illustrated page with verse from *Baby Days*, 1880, by Amy Neally with illustrations by Ida Waugh, Eddie J. Andrews, and Harriett M. Bennett, published by E. P. Dutton & Co., New York.

Baby at seashore, an illustrated page from *Baby Days*, 1880, by Amy Neally with illustrations by Ida Waugh, Eddie J. Andrews, and Harriett M. Bennett, published by E. P. Dutton & Co., New York.

Blue decorated cover from *All About Me, Baby's Record,* 1918, by Josephine Wheeler Weage. Published by Saalfield Co., Akron. Book, $75-125.

"My Daily Nap," an illustrated page from *All About Me, Baby's Record,* 1918, by Josephine Wheeler Weage, published by Saalfield Co., Akron.

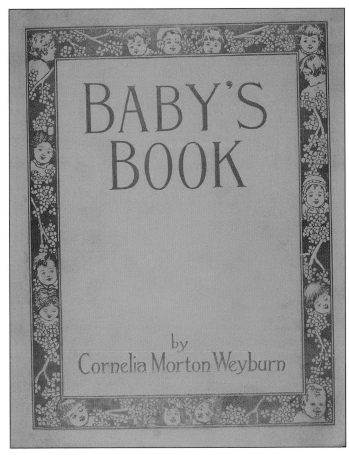

Pink cover from *Baby's Book,* c. 1910, by Cornelia Morton
Weyburn with verses by Francis Buzzell, published by Barse
& Hopkins, New York. Book, $75-150.

Decorated title page from *Baby's Book,* c. 1910, by
Cornelia Morton Weyburn with verses by Francis
Buzzell, published by Barse & Hopkins, New York.

"First Christmas," an illustrated page from *Baby's Book*, c. 1910, by Cornelia Morton Weyburn with verses by Frances Buzzell, published by Barse & Hopkins, New York.

Title page with stork and baby in doctor's bag from *Mother Stork's Baby Book,* 1904, by Albertine Randall Wheelan, published by the Dodge Company, New York. Book, $100-200.

Decorated table of contents page from *Mother Stork's Baby Book*, 1904, by Albertine Randall Wheelan, published by the Dodge Company, New York.

Contents.

"Record of Life," illustrated page from *Mother Stork's Baby Book*, 1904, by Albertine Randall Wheelan, published by the Dodge Company, New York.

Poem by Eugene Field on decorated page from *Mother Stork's Baby Book*, 1904, by Albertine Randall Wheelan, published by the Dodge Company, New York.

THE BOTTLE TREE
BY EUGENE FIELD

A BOTTLE TREE bloometh in Winkyway land —
Heigh-ho for a bottle, I say!
A snug little berth in that ship I demand
That rocketh the Bottle-Tree babies away
Where the Bottle Tree bloometh by night and by day
And reacheth its fruit to each wee, dimpled hand;
You take of that fruit as much as you list,
For colic's a nuisance that does n't exist!
So cuddle me close, and cuddle me fast,
And cuddle me snug in my cradle away,
For I hunger and thirst for that precious repast —
Heigh-ho for a bottle, I say!

"The Bottle Tree," a poem and decorated page from *Mother Stork's Baby Book,* 1904, by Albertine Randall Wheelan, published by the Dodge Company, New York.

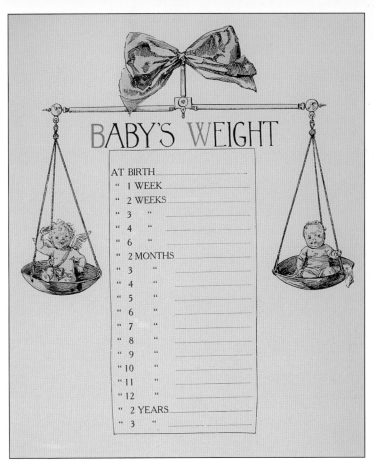

"Baby's Weight," illustrated page from *Mother Stork's Baby Book,* 1904, by Albertine Randall Wheelan, published by the Dodge Company, New York.

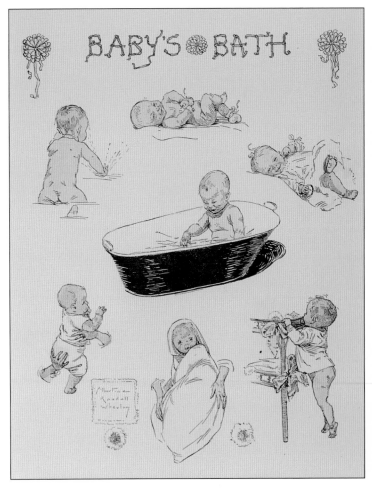

"Baby's Bath," an illustrated page from *Mother Stork's Baby Book,* 1904, by Albertine Randall Wheelan, published by the Dodge Company, New York.

Say, what is the spell, when her fledglings are cheeping,
That lures the bird home to her nest?
Or wakes the tired mother whose infant is weeping,
To cuddle and croon it to rest?
What the magic that charms the glad babe in her arms
Till it cooes with the voice of a dove?
'Tis a secret, and so let us whisper it low—
And the name of the secret is Love!
For I think it is Love,
For I feel it is Love,
For I'm sure it is nothing but Love!

Lewis Carroll.

Poem by Lewis Carroll on illustrated page from *Mother Stork's Baby Book*, 1904,
by Albertine Randall Wheelan, published by the Dodge Company, New York.

GARDEN AND CRADLE.

EUGENE FIELD.

WHEN our babe he goeth walking in his garden,
   Around his tinkling feet the sunbeams play;
The posies they are good to him
   And bow them as they should to him,
As fareth he upon his kingly way;
   And birdlings of the wood to him
   Make music, gentle music, all the day,
When our babe he goeth walking in his garden.

WHEN our babe he goeth swinging in his cradle,
   Then the night it looketh ever sweetly down:
The little stars are kind to him,
   The moon she hath a mind to him
And layeth on his head a golden crown;
   And singeth then the wind to him
   A song, the gentle song of Bethlem-town,
When our babe he goeth swinging in his cradle.

"Garden and Cradle," a poem by Eugene Field on illustrated page from *Mother Stork's Baby Book*, 1904, by Albertine Randall Wheelan, published by the Dodge Company, New York.

Pink decorated cover from *Little Baby's Big Days*, 1916, by Edith Truman Woolf, published by C. R. Gibson & Co., New York. Book, $75-150.

Title page with decoration from *Little Baby's Big Days*, 1916, by Edith Truman Woolf, published by C. R. Gibson & Co., New York.

Decorated cover from *All About Baby,* c. 1890. No author, illustrator, or publisher noted. $75-125.

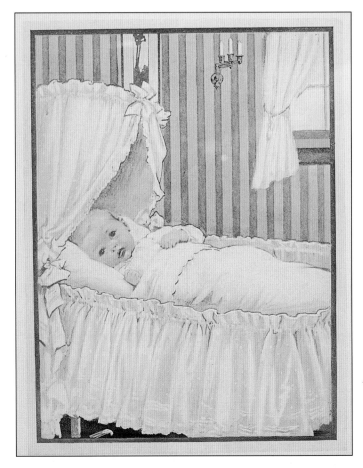

Baby in crib, an illustrated page from *My Biography,* 1914, published by The Bordens Condensed Milk Co., New York. Book, $50-125.

Mother and child, an illustrated page from *My Biography*, 1914,
published by The Bordens Condensed Milk Co., New York.

Mother and children, an illustrated page from *My Biography*, 1914,
published by The Bordens Condensed Milk Co., New York.

Mitigates annoyances of travelling.

Mother and child traveling, an illustrated page from *My Biography,*
1914, published by The Bordens Condensed Milk Co., New York.

Mother feeding child, an illustrated page from *My Biography*, 1914,
published by the Bordens Condensed Milk Co., New York.

Chapter Three

The Babies

Over half of the baby books in this collection contain information about a baby born between 1880 and 1930. In some cases, we have a book filled to the brim with information, notes, pictures, hair, the baby's booties, telegrams, tags from the baby's first Christmas, tags from the baby's first birthday, family trees, and much, much more. In other cases, we have only a few bits of family information.

The oldest baby is Frances Mae Cook, born in Plainfield, New Jersey on May 12, 1883. Her baby information was recorded in *The Baby's Journal* by S. Alice Bray. Two others were born in the 1880s: Mary Grimes Cowper on January 1, 1889 and Ruth Fowler on June 19, 1889 in Fremont, Nebraska. Eight babies were born in the 1890s.

The pictures from their baby books serve several purposes. First, you will become acquainted with the baby and its family. Second, you will discover that every mother recorded information in her own unique way. Third, you will see the wonderfully decorated pages by the illustrators and their wide array of styles.

Here are the babies:

Baby: Madeline Eleanor Almy

Born: Friday, February 26, 1897 at 11:00 PM in New Bedford, Massachusetts

Father: Norman Q. Almy

Mother: Madeline Eleanor Almy

Baby Book: *The Baby's Biography*, 1891, by A. O. Kaplan and illustrated by Frances Brundage

Dedication in book: To Madeline Eleanor Almy from Aunt Harriet

Poem: A handwritten poem by A. G. C. to M. E. A., dated March 28, 1897

Booties: This book contains Madeline's first ivory and blue booties.

Comment: Madeline's mother filled her baby books with lists of baby gifts, list of first Christmas gifts, a lock of her hair, and many wonderful notes and comments.

Baby: Margaret Randolph "Peggy" Armstrong

Born: December 3, 1922 at 7:35 PM at the Good Samaritan Hospital

Father: Lionel Armstrong

Mother: Meekin Armstrong

Baby Book: *Mother Stork's Baby Book, 1904,* by Albertine Randall Wheelan

Her baby book is filled with photographs, her mother's wonderful notes, nine telegrams in a pasted in envelope, eleven greeting cards, and a package of family letters.

"This is Record of the Life of Margaret Randolph Armstrong" page from *Mother Stork's Baby Book,* 1904, by Albertine Randall Wheelan.

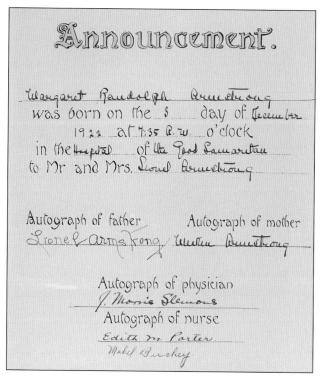

Announcement page for Margaret "Peggy" Randolph Armstrong, born on December 3, 1922 at 7:35 PM at the Good Samaritan Hospital to Mr. & Mrs. Lionel Armstrong.

BABY'S FIRST PHOTOGRAPH
2 months

If thou couldst know thine own sweetness,
O little one, perfect and sweet,
Thou wouldst be a child forever;
Completer whilst incomplete.

Francis Turner Palgrave.

Baby's first photograph at two months:
Margaret "Peggy" Randolph Armstrong.

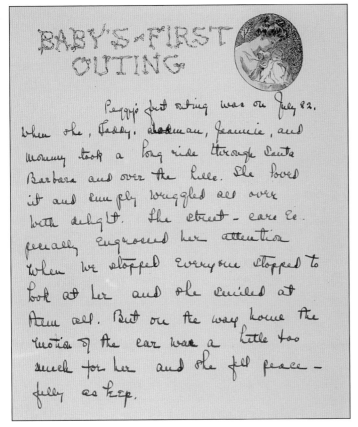

BABY'S FIRST OUTING

Peggy's first outing was on July 22. When she, Daddy, Grandman, Jeannie, and Mommy took a long ride through Santa Barbara and over the hills. She loved it and simply wriggled all over with delight. The street-cars especially engrossed her attention. When we stopped everyone stopped to look at her and she smiled at them all. But on the way home the motion of the car was a little too much for her and she fell peacefully asleep.

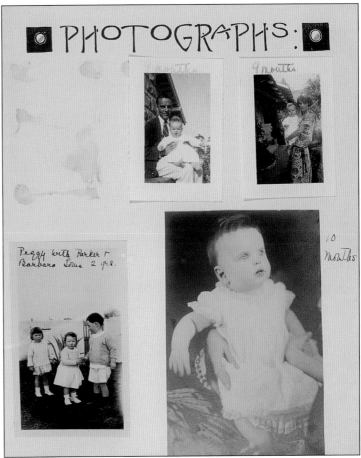

PHOTOGRAPHS:

Peggy with Parker + Barbara Louis 2 yrs.

10 months

Photographs of Peggy Armstrong: at nine months with
father; at nine months with mother; at ten months;
and at two years with Parker and Barbara Louis.

Baby's first outing on July 22, 1923: a
pony ride through the Santa Barbara,
California, hills. Peggy fell asleep!

Baby: Suzanne Auch

Born: Monday, September 27, 1915 at 3:00 PM in Kokomo, Indiana

Father: Charles J. Auch

Mother: Loraine A. Auch

Baby Book: *Baby's Biography, 1913,* by Clara M. Burd

Comment: Suzanne's baby book is filled! Nearly every page is completed. There is a list of first presents, a lock of her hair, list of first visitors, baby's first photograph, photo of her home, photo of her parents, and endless notes by her mother. Laid in the book is her Cradle Roll Certificate from the Congregational Sunday School dated November 9, 1918.

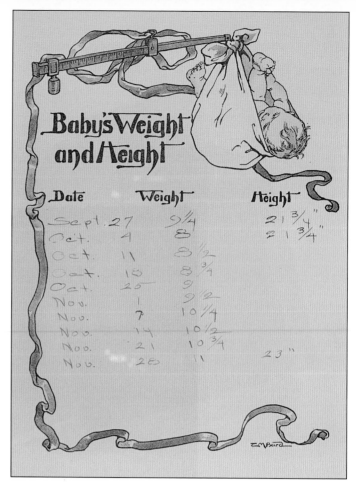

Suzanne Auch's baby height and weight page.

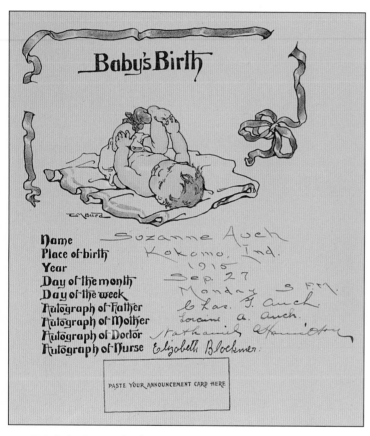

Baby's birth page for Suzanne Auch, born on Monday, September 27, 1915 at 3:00 PM in Kokomo, Indiana. Her baby information is found in *Baby's Biography, 1913,* by Clara M. Burd.

Baby: Carlos Cornelius Banting, Jr.

Born: January 9, 1915

Residence: 2455 Robinwood Avenue, Toledo, Ohio

Baby Book: *Baby Days, A Sunbonnet Record, 1910,* by Bertha L. Corbett

Comment: His book has only the Baby's Record page completed, at one week he weighed eight pounds, and on the Best Loved Pets page is recorded the word: *"Chummire."*

And that is all we know about Carlos!

Carlos Cornelius Banting, Jr. was born on January 9, 1915 at his parent's residence at 2455 Robinwood Avenue, Toledo, Ohio. His baby information is recorded in *Baby Days, A Sunbonnet Record, 1910,* by Bertha C. Corbett.

Baby: Thomas Jefferson Bayuhaw

Born: January 30, 1913 at Providence, Kentucky

Father: R. G. Bayuhaw

Mother: Vara Ford Bayuhaw

Baby Book: *Baby's Book,* 1910, by Cornelia Morton Weyburn

Note: We are not sure if we have the baby's last name spelled correctly; the script has been deciphered several ways.

Comment: Many pages have been completed by his mother in the first half of the book including first outing, first laugh, first shoes, et cetera.

Family Trees: On this father's side, we know that Thomas' great grandfather was Thomas B. Jefferson. On his mother's side, we know that his great grandfathers were Patrick Harvey Ford and John Henry Blane.

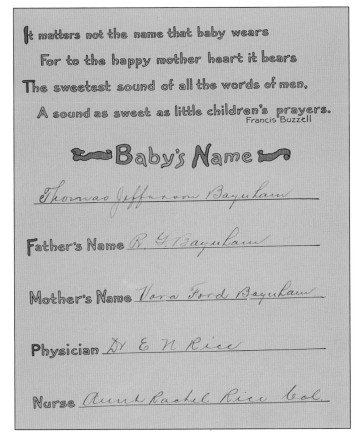

Thomas Jefferson Bayuham (maybe, Bayuhaw) was born on January 30, 1913 in Providence, Kentucky. His baby information was recorded in a *Baby's Book,* 1910, by Cornelia Morton Weyburn.

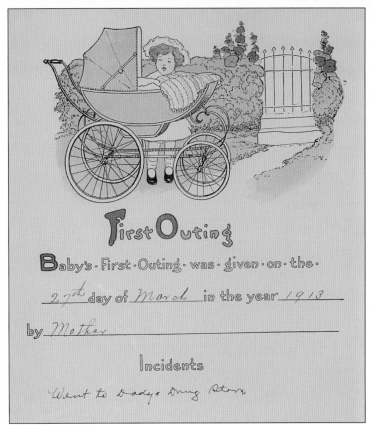

Thomas Bayuham. At the age of two months, Thomas was taken by his mother on his first outing. He went "to Dady's Drug Store."

Thomas Bayuham. On April 7, we have a record of Thomas's first laugh.

First Lock of Hair

= = = = =

The First Lock of Hair was Clipped by *Miss McKim*

Friend on the *First* day of

May in the year of *1914* when

Baby was *Fifteen months* old.

Thomas Bayuham. The first lock of clipped hair
was cut at the age of fifteen months.

Announcement.

Margaret Faucher Bohn
was born on the *12th* day of *February*
19 *11* at *11 57 PM* o'clock
in the *home* of
to Mr and Mrs *William Bernhard Bohn*

Autograph of father   Autograph of mother
                                Mrs. Wm. B. Bohn

Autograph of physician

Autograph of nurse
Elizabeth Pole Clapp

Margaret Faucher Bohn was born at home on February 12, 1911 at
11:57 PM. Margaret's baby history was recorded in a *Mother
Stork's Baby Book* by Albertine Randall Wheelan.

Baby: Ralph Coonley Blessing
Born: September 18, 1901
Father: Elwood G. Blessing
Mother: Anna Blanche Coonley Blessing
Baby Book: *Baby's Record,* 1898, by Maud
Humphrey
Comment: This baby book was completed from beginning to the end by his mother, including photographs and a lock of baby hair.

Baby: Margaret Faucher Bohn
Born: February 12, 1911 at 11:57 PM at home
Father: William Bernhard Bohn
Baby Book: *Mother Stork's Baby Book,* 1904, by
Albertine Randall Wheelan
Comment: In Margaret's baby book, we find only a few pages filled out: her name, her first outing, announcement, and a 1913 telegram laid in the book

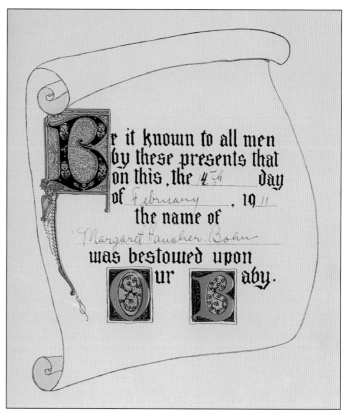

*e it known to all men
by these presents that
on this, the *4th* day
of *February*, 19 *11*
the name of
Margaret Faucher Bohn
was bestowed upon
*O*ur *B*aby.

Margaret Faucher Bohn. The beautifully decorated
Name Is Given page for Margaret.

Baby: Howard Spencer Bray

Born: October 9, 1919 at Haverhill, Massachusetts

Baby Book: *Baby Days, A Sunbonnet Record,* 1910, by Bertha L. Corbett

Comment: Only a few bits of baby record were completed, including weight of seven pounds at birth, blue eyes, brown hair, first tooth on June 3, 1920 and first word "Dady."

Howard Spencer Bray was born on October 9, 1919 at Haverhill, Massachusetts. He weighted seven pounds and two ounces. His baby information was recorded in a *Baby Days: A Sunbonnet Record,* by Bertha L. Corbett.

Baby: Carol DeWitt Bridgman

Born: July 30, 1906

Father: Theodore H. Bridgman

Mother: Addie Wilson Bridgman

Baby Book: *Baby's Record,* 1898, by Maud Humphrey

Comment: The first half of her baby book was nicely filled in with her baby records, including Christening at Holy Trinity Church, first outing, weight, first gifts, first tooth and much, much more.

Baby: Frederick William Broderick, Jr.

Born: November 14, 1930

Father: Frederick William Broderick, born December 7, 1904, Oakland, California

Mother: Marie Pauline Barbour Broderick, born March 11, 1905

Baby Book: *Baby's Own Book,* 1923, by S. F. Farini

Comment: This small baby book contains valuable family history of Frederick, family photos, baby notes, a dozen Christmas gift tags pasted in, and much more.

Frederick William Broderick, Jr. was born on November 14, 1930. His baby information was recorded in *Baby's Own Book,* by S. F. Farini.

Photo of Frederick William Broderick, Jr. with sister.

Frederick William Broderick, Jr. has a first merry Christmas. His mother pasted into his baby book some of the Christmas tags.

Baby: Conrad Ainsworth Burpee

Born: November 13, 1898
Father: Harry Howard Burpee
Mother: Nettie Frances Ainsworth Burpee
Baby Book: *Baby's Record,* 1898, by Maud Humphrey

Comment: His baby book has a few items filled in, including first outing, weight, first tooth and a baby photograph.

Conrad Ainsworth Burpee was born on November 13, 1898. His baby book was *Baby's Record,* by Maud Humphrey.

Frederick William Broderick, Jr. has a younger sister. This is her picture from his baby book.

Conrad Ainsworth Burpee has his first photograph taken.

Baby: Donald Alfred Cameron, Jr.

    Born: February 24, 1910
    Father: Donald Alfred Cameron
    Mother: Mary J. Cameron
    Baby Book: *Baby's Record*, 1898, by Maud Humphrey

    Comment: Only a few pages were ever filled in, including his weight, first gifts, first short clothes and First Christmas.

Baby: Frank Edward Caskey

    Born: Monday, October 23, 1916 at 12:30 AM.
    Baby Book: *Baby*, no date, no author, nor publisher
    Comment: In addition to his name and date of birth, his baby book contains only his weight of ten pounds at birth and thirteen pounds at two weeks.

Frank Edward Caskey was born on Monday, October 23, 1916 at 12:30 AM. His baby book was *Baby*, c. 1916, no author. This is the cover of his baby book with its hand painted "baby."

Baby: Evelyn Goodman Coleman

    Born: January 27, 1908 at 8:30, at home
    Mother: Elizabeth Coleman
    Baby Book: *Baby's Book*, c. 1905, by Frances Brundage and M. Bowley

    Comment: Her mother filled Evelyn's baby book with lists of gifts, first visitors, first outing on March 18, 1908 with her mother and daddy, Valentines pasted in, two letters, and Christmas tags.

Baby: Thomas Junior Connolly

    Born: September 1, 1902
    Father: Thomas Edward Connolly
    Mother: Ida Louise Connolly
    Baby Book: *Baby's Book*, c. 1900, by Ida Scott Taylor and illustrated by Frances Brundage

    Comment: His baby book was completed with his first photograph, list of baby gifts, his first Valentines pasted in, and much more.

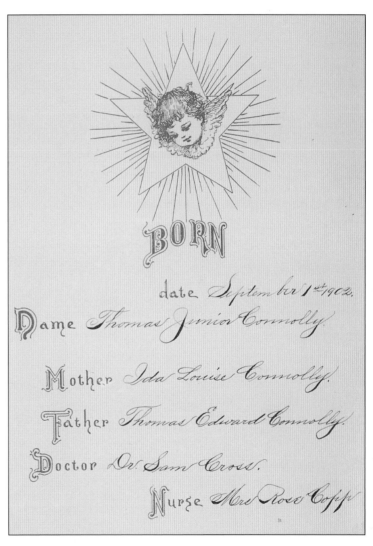

Thomas Junior Connolly was born on September 1, 1902. His baby information is contained in *Baby's Book*, by Frances Brundage.

Thomas Junior Connolly. His first baby picture.

Baby: Leah Anne Conrad

Born: November 3, 1929, at 5:00 AM, in Springville, Pennsylvania

Father: L. F. Conrad

Mother: Harriett Conrad

Baby Book: *My Baby's Book*, 1927, by E. Schacherer

Comment: Her baby book is partially completed with a list of gifts, messages, and a list of her relatives.

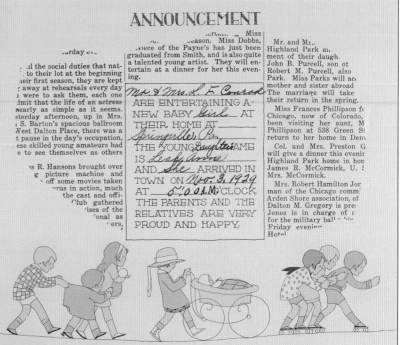

Leah Anne Conrad was born on November 3, 1929 in Springville, Pennsylvania. Her baby information was recorded in a *My Baby's Book*, by E. Schacherer.

Baby: Florence Mae Cook

Born: May 12, 1883 in Plainfield, New Jersey

Baby Book: *The Baby's Journal,* 1882, by S. Alice Bray

Comment: Her mother recorded her baby record on four pages and listed her first gifts. Her first photograph is pasted in.

Thomas Junior Connolly. On March 1. 1903, he wore his first short clothes.

Florence Mae Cook was born on May 12, 1883 in Plainfield, New Jersey. Her baby information was recorded in *The Baby's Journal,* by S. Alice Bray.

Florence Mae Cook, perhaps her first photograph.

Baby: Mary Grimes Cowper

Born: January 1, 1889

Baby Book: *The Baby's Journal,* 1885, by S. Alice Bray

Comment: On a single page we find information about Mary and her brother, Bryan, who was born on April 19, 1890. Locks of hair from both children are pinned to the page.

Special Comment: Included with her baby book was a second, handmade booklet, *My Wish for the Baby,* which contains an original poem!

Mary Grimes Cowper was born on January 1, 1889. Her baby information is found in *The Baby's Journal,* by S. Alice Bray.

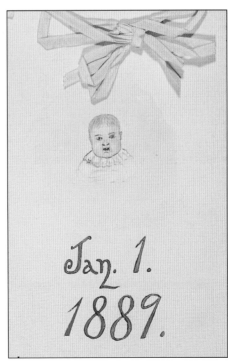

Mary Grimes Cowper. This is the cover of a handmade baby record book which came with her baby book.

Baby: Lionel Burton Davidson

Born: November 4, 1932, London

Father: L. M. Davidson

Mother: E. M. Davidson

Baby Book: *Baby's Record,* 1928, by Anne Anderson

Comment: There are only a few entries in Lionel's baby book.

Baby: Harold Lee De Ford

Born: September 11, 1910 at 7:00 PM at home, Kansas City, Missouri

Father: Lee De Ford

Mother: May De Ford

Baby Book: *Our Baby,* c. 1900. No author or illustrator.

Comment: One of Harold's first gifts was $5.00 from Grandpa Owings

Baby: Mildred Louise Fisher

Born: April 21, 1902

Father: Earle F. Fisher

Mother: Cordie C. Fisher

Baby Book: *Baby's Record,* 1898, by Maud Humphrey

Comment: Her large baby book is filled with information from front to back, including locks of hair, several first Valentines pasted in, and many baby and family photographs.

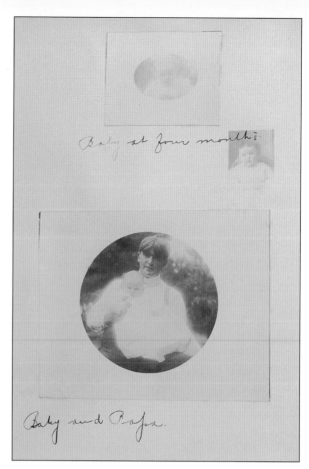

Mildred Louise Fisher's first baby photograph and a later photo with her father, Earle F. Fisher.

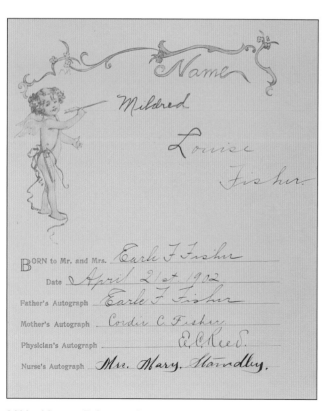

Mildred Louise Fisher was born on April 21, 1902. Her baby records were recorded in *Baby's Record,* by Maud Humphrey.

Mildred Louise Fisher at one year and two years.

Baby: Margaret Fletcher

Born: April 23, 1915 at Temple, Texas
Father: Rev. Custis Fletcher
Mother: Margaret Mary Cresley Fletcher
Baby Book: *Baby Days, A Sunbonnet Record,* 1910, by Bertha L. Corbett

Comment: Her mother made entries on most of the pages including Christening, first creeping, first tooth, record of unusual events, and much more.

Baby: Ruth Fowler

Born: Wednesday, June 19, 1889 at Fremont, Nebraska
Baby Book: *The Baby's Journal,* 1885, by S. Alice Bray

Comment: The only information recorded in her baby book was her weight and teeth records.

Ruth Fowler was born on Wednesday, June 19, 1889 at 5:50 AM at Fremont, Nebraska. Her baby record was recorded in *The Baby's Journal,* by S. Alice Bray.

Baby: Robert "Bobby" Lewis Gade

Born: Saturday, November 8, 1919
Father: G. L. Gade
Baby Book: *The Book of Baby Mine,* 1915, by Melcena Burns Denny

Comment: This baby book is filled with notes, family information, and baby and family photographs.

Margaret Fletcher was born on April 23, 1915 at the Temple Sanitarium in Temple, Texas. Her baby records were recorded in *Baby Days, A Sunbonnet Record,* by Bertha L. Corbett.

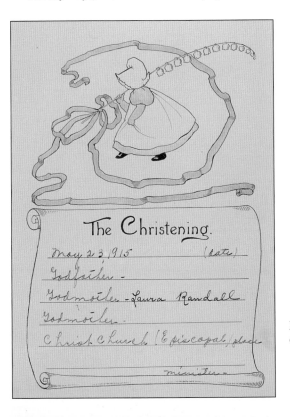

Margaret Fletcher was christened on May 23, 1915.

Robert Lewis "Bobby" Gade was born on Saturday, November 8, 1919. His baby record was recorded in *The Book of Baby Mine,* by Melcena Burns Denny.

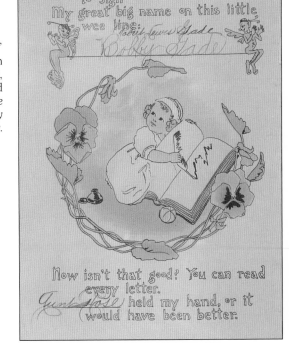

Dear Doctor, I know you are
busy, but maybe
you will sign on this line, just
to please a good baby?

And nurse, here's a line that
was meant just for you.
If the fairies annoy you, just
say to them, "Shoo!"

Bobby Gade. This is a picture of his home on a lovely decorated page from his baby book.

Photographs

Age - 5 months.

Bobby Gade, his photograph at five months old.

Baby: Gordon Monroe Harrison Gadeberg
    Born: Monday, December 1, 1913
    Father: G. W. Gadeberg
    Mother: Laura C. Gadeberg
    Baby Book: *Our Baby*, 1909, by Frances Brundage and May Sandheim
    Comment: Gordon's baby book was nicely filled in with information, including a wonderful photograph of mother and baby.
    Special Comment: Father saw his son for the first time on December 21, 1913.

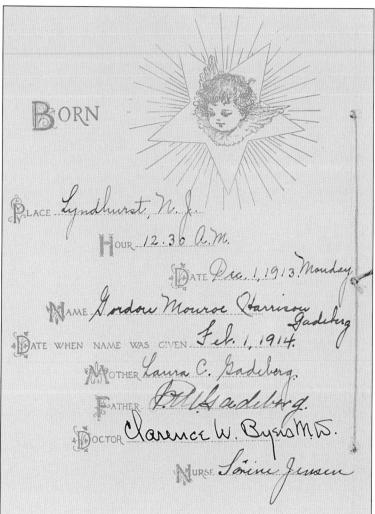

Gordon Monroe Harrison Gadeberg was born on December 1, 1913. His baby record was recorded in *Our Baby*, by Frances Brundage and May Sandheim.

Gordon Gadeberg and his mother in his first photograph.

Baby: **Robert Austin Greer**

Born: Thursday, May 7, 1936 at 5:55 PM
Father: Justin M. Greer
Mother: Helen C. Greer
Baby Book: *The Book of Baby Mine*, 1935 (1915), by Melcena Burns Denny

Comment: Robert's baby book contains many notations including his first journey and first days at school.

Robert Austin Greer was born on Thursday, May 7, 1936 at 5:55 PM. His baby record was recorded in *The Book of Baby Mine*, by Melcena Burns Denny. This beautifully decorated page displaying his father's family tree is from his baby book.

Baby: Doris Fae Guynes

Born: January 30, 1921 at 8:00 AM in the City of Bonham, Texas
Father: H. H. Guynes
Mother: Gladys Fae Guynes
Baby Book: *Babyhood Days*, 1915, by Jessie Alma Pierson

Comment: Her baby book has many pages completed with interesting information, including her father's family tree and mother's family tree. It ends with her first day at school on September 19, 1927.

Doris Fae Guynes was born on January 30, 1921. Her baby record was recorded in *Babyhood Days*, by Jessie Alma Pierson.

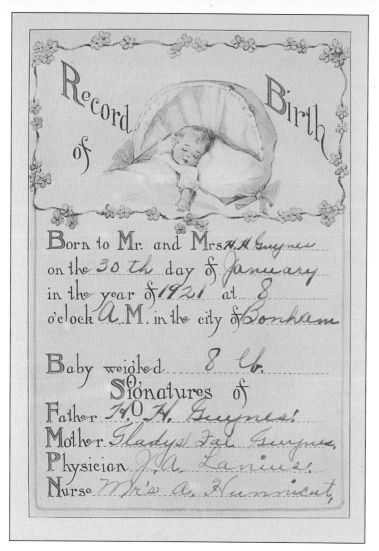

Record of Birth

Born to Mr. and Mrs. H. H. Guynes
on the 30th day of January
in the year of 1921 at 8
o'clock A.M. in the city of Bonham

Baby weighed 8 lb.

Signatures of
Father H. H. Guynes,
Mother Gladys Fae Guynes,
Physician J. A. Lanius,
Nurse Mrs. A. Hunnicut,

Doris Fae Guynes's record of her birth was
recorded on a lovely decorated page.

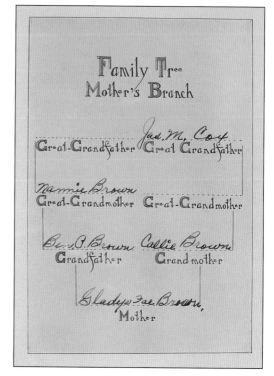

Doris Guynes' Family Tree Mother's Branch page.

Family Tree
Mother's Branch

| Great-Grandfather | Jas. M. Cox Great-Grandfather |
| Nannie Brown Great-Grandmother | Great-Grandmother |

Ben P. Brown Grandfather — Callie Brown Grandmother

Gladys Fae Brown, Mother

Doris Guynes' Family Tree
Father's Branch page.

Family Tree
Father's Branch

N. M. Guynes Great-Grandfather — A. Lasater Great-Grandfather

Caroline Guynes Great-Grandmother — Kesia Lasater Great-Grandmother

J. B. Guynes Grandfather — Sarah Guynes Grandmother

H. H. Guynes Father

Baby: Alleen Ames Hamilton

Born: February 19, 1895

Baby Book: *The Baby's Journal,* 1895, by S. Alice Bray

Comment: This baby journal has only a couple of blank pages for baby information to be entered. On a single page we learn that Alleen took her first ride by rail on December 25, 1895 and her first tooth came on November 29, 1895.

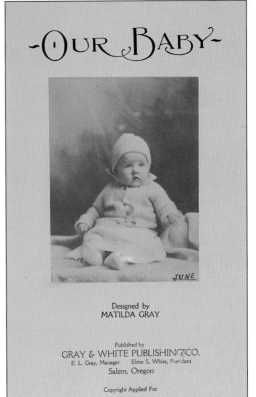

Designed by
MATILDA GRAY

Published by
GRAY & WHITE PUBLISHING CO.
E. L. Gray, Manager   Elmo S. White, President
Salem, Oregon

Copyright Applied For

June Heppner's first photograph in *Our Baby,* by Matilda Gray.

Aileen Ames Hamilton was born on February 19, 1895. Her baby records were recorded in *The Baby's Journal,* by S. Alice Bray.

Baby: Laureus Hammond

Born: Friday, January 11, 1895 at 12:20 AM

Father: William Andrew Hammong

Mother: Idea Strong Hamilton

Baby Book: *The Baby's Biography,* 1891, by A. O. Kaplan with illustrations by Frances Brundage

Comment: Some events were noted by his mother in a very soft handwriting.

Baby: June Heppner

Born: June 4, 1926

Father: Peter Heppner

Mother: Lydia Heppner

Baby Book: *Our Baby,* c. 1920, designed by Matilda Gray

Comment: On the title page, there is a photo of June. Many pages were filled out by her mother including a nice family tree.

June Heppner was born on June 4, 1926 in Salem, Oregon.

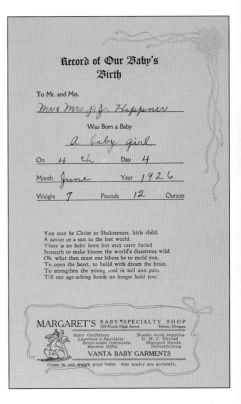

Baby: Margaret Hess

Born: Saturday, March 30, 1907 at 12:45 PM
Parents: Mr. & Mrs. Alfred F. Hess
Baby Book: *The Baby's Biography,* 1891, by A. O. Kaplan with illustrations by Frances Brundage
Comment: Some of the pages have been completed in Margaret's baby book. A weekly record of her weight was recorded on one page for the first 52 weeks. Laid in the book is a handwritten diet and feeding schedule.

Baby: Norma Marie Hobbs

Born: June 16, 1907 at 4:10 PM
Father: George R. Hobbs
Mother: Irma Natalie Knapp Hobbs
Baby Book: *Baby's Book,* c. 1900, by Ida Scott Taylor with illustrations by Frances Brundage
Comment: Norma's mother completed every page in her baby book with dates and events. Her first little shoe was a present from Aunt Carrie at about three months.

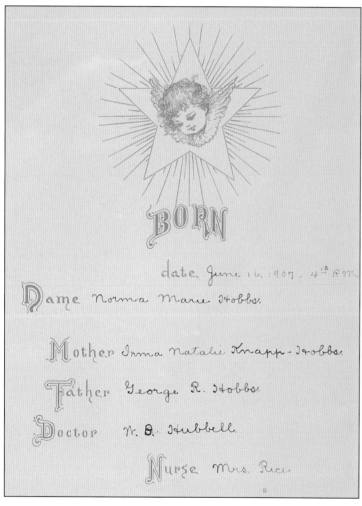

Norma Marie Hobbs was born on June 16, 1907 at 4:10 PM. Her baby records were recorded in *Baby's Book,* by Frances Brundage.

An early photograph in the young life of Elinor Margaret Holmes.

Baby: Elinor Margaret Holmes

Born: January 6, 1916 in Washington, DC
Father: Patrick Douglas Holmes
Mother: Gertrude Elizabeth Holmes
Baby Book: *Baby's Record,* 1898, by Maud Humphrey
Comment: Only a few pages were completed in Elinor's baby book. However, there are two baby photographs with her parents plus a detailed record of two dozen baby gifts with the senders' names.

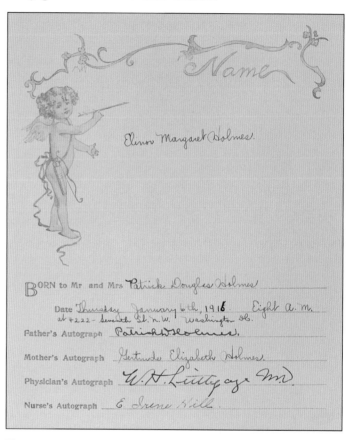

Elinor Margaret Holmes was born on January 6, 1916. She and her parents lived in Washington, D.C. Her baby record was recorded in *Baby's Record,* by Maud Humphrey.

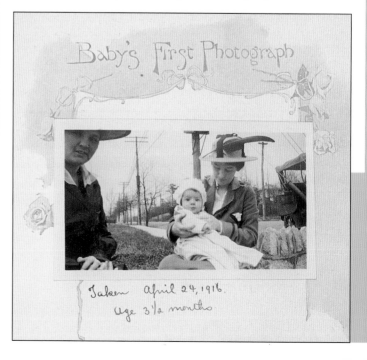

Another photograph of Elinor Margaret Holmes.

Baby: Josephine Hutchin

Born: not known

Baby Book: *The Baby's Journal,* 1885, by S. Alice Bray

Comment: This baby book contains only the following inscription on the front end-page: *"Josephine Hutchins, xmas 1900, Aunt Jewel."*

Baby: Lilian Beatrice Julia Jeffrey

Born: Wednesday, December 6, 1922 at 6:30 AM at Les Ormen Teddington, Middlesex, England

Father: Robert Riddle Jeffrey

Mother: Lillian B. Jeffrey

Baby Book: *Baby's Souvenir,* c. 1910, by A. O. Kaplan with illustrations by Frances Brundage (On the cover of this London edition, Frances Brundage's name was misspelled "Brondage".)

Comment: Lilian's baby book has notations and information throughout the whole book: her first laugh on January 16, 1923, an origin poem "To Jewel" handwritten by E. F. G. R. on January 19, 1923, and two gold sovereigns on Merry Christmas Day.

Special Comment: Laid into the book is Lilian's Christening Record: January 14, 1923 at home, signed by the Vicar.

Baby: Graham Starr Jones

Born: November 9, 1909 at 10:00 in Webb City

Father: Judson Waldo Jones

Mother: Elsie Starr Jones

Baby Book: *Mother Stork's Baby Book,* 1904, by Albertine Randall Wheelan

Comment: Very little was ever written in Graham's baby book. There are little scraps of paper laid in with bits of information here and there.

Baby: John Eyford Kennedy

Born: Sunday, January 20, 1918, Minneapolis, Minnesota

Father: Jack F. Kennedy

Baby Book: *Baby's Own Book,* c. 1910, no author, illustrator or publisher

Baby: Johnny Frank Lemmons

Born: January 29, 1930, Dallas, Texas

Father: Leon J. Lemmons

Mother: Velma Lemmons

Baby Book: *The Dear Baby,* c, 1920, no author, illustrator or publisher

Comment: Johnny's baby book is filled to the brim with notes, photographs of baby and family, and baby cards.

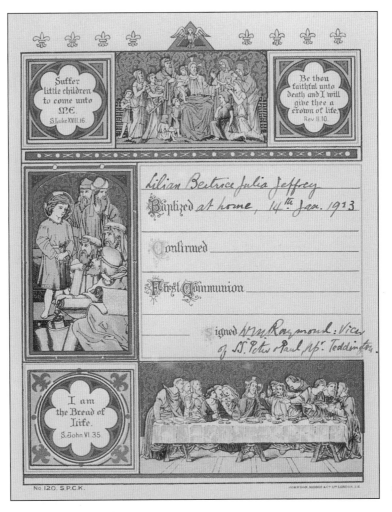

Lilian Beatrice Julia Jeffrey was born on Wednesday, December 6, 1922 at 6:30 AM at Les Ormen Teddington, Middlesex. Her baby record was recorded in *Baby's Souvenir,* by A. O. Kaplan and illustrated by Frances Brundage. This is her baptismal record which was included in her baby book.

Baby: Eirene Stella Maurice Luckraft

Born: October 21, 1923 at 6:40 PM
Father: Rev. Lawrence Charles Luckraft
Mother: Ethel Luckraft
Baby Book: *A Record of Our Baby,* 1921, by Meta Morris Grimball

Comment: This is a small baby book which is filled with notes, photographs, and a lock of hair. Included with her baby book was a twelve month engagement book for the year 1921 with many notations referring to her older brother Rex perhaps.

Eirene Stella Maurice Luckraft was born on October 21, 1923 at 6:40 PM in London. Her father was Rev. Lawrence Charles Luckraft. Her baby record was recorded in *A Record of Our Baby,* by Meta Morris Grimball.

Baby: Robert Clark McCormack

Born: Thursday, May 19, 1898 at 4:40 PM *"on a rainy day"*
Father: Fletcher Andrew McCormack
Mother: May Clark McCormack
Baby Book: *Baby's Book,* c. 1895, by Ida Scott Taylor with illustrations by Frances Brundage

Comment: Robert's mother filled in every page available with notes and comments which often wound their way to the back of the next page. Robert was christened at the First Congregational Church, Sioux Falls, Iowa on the Second of October.

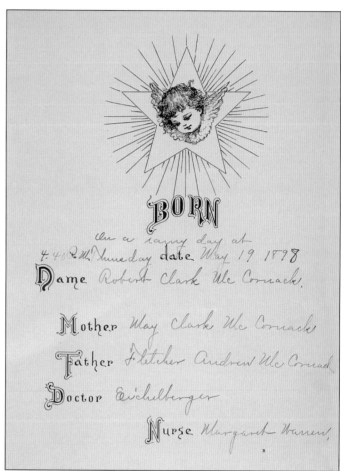

Robert Clark McCormack was born on May 19, 1898. His baby record was recorded in *Baby's Book,* by Frances Brundage.

From the photograph page, four photos of Eirene Luckraft.

Illustrated "First little Shoes" page for Robert McCormack, with his mother's notes at the bottom of the page.

Illustrated "First Short Clothes" page for Robert McCormack, with his mother's notes at the top of the page.

Illustrated "First Word" page for Robert McCormack, with his mother's notes.

Baby: Hazel Elizabeth McDonald

Born: April 18, 1918 in Pepperell, Massachusetts

Baby Book: *Baby Days, A Sunbonnet Record,* 1910, by Bertha L. Corbett

Comment: Hazel's baby book has few notations. She did get her first ring from Aunt Lida and a doll from *grandma* on December 25, 1918, her first Christmas.

Hazel Elizabeth McDonald was born on April 18, 1918 in Pepperell, Massachusetts. Her baby record was recorded in Baby's Days, A Sunbonnet Record, by Bertha L. Corbett.

Baby: Baby McNawee

Born: Sunday, May 25, 1902 at home in Kewerhood Village

Parents: Mr. & Mrs. Frederick McNawee

Baby Book: *Baby's Red Letter Days*, 1901, by Jessie Wilcox Smith

Comment: Only a single page was filled in: the "Baby is Born" page.

Baby: Louise Emily Maier

Born: Sunday, March 3, 1918 at 7:45 AM. Dorchester, Massachusetts

Baby Book: *Baby's Book, A Record*, 1916, by Florence Choate and Elizabeth Curtis

Comment: "On March 17, 1918, Louise was taken in an automobile by her Aunt Emily and Papa and Big Sister Elsa to the Zions Lutheran Church in Boston – where Uncle Walter christened her."

Baby: Leonard Ernest Neale

Born: Friday, January 8, 1904 at 3:30 PM in Baltimore, Maryland at home

Parents: Dr. & Mrs. Leonard Ernest Neale

Baby Book: *Baby's Biography*, 1891, by A. O. Kapland with illustrations by Frances Brundage

Comment: In addition to the above information from the "Welcome Little Stranger" page, we only have his weight of seven pounds on January 8, 1904.

Baby: Eugene Henry Nichols

Born: August 21, 1914 at 5 AM

Father: Samuel Henry Nichols

Mother: Alta Iva Nichols

Baby Book: *Baby's Book*, c. 1900, by Ida Scott Taylor with illustrations by Frances Brundage

Comment: Most of Eugene's baby book is completed, including a notation by his mother that on his first birthday he "had cake baked. Crawled to bread box and took it our and laid it on the floor beside the box and pinched out a piece."

Illustrated "First little Shoes" page for Eugene Nichol. The shoes were white and he was five months old.

Baby: Anne Chawpe Orr

Born: August 2, 1899

Father: J. H. Orr

Mother: Anne Chawpe Orr

Baby Book: *Baby's Book*, c. 1895, by Ida Scott Taylor with illustrations by Frances Brundage

Comment: Her father passed away at home in January of 1902. Her mother recorded some of the events of her two-year-old daughter during that month in her baby book. "She continually asked about him and on January 26th she said that she wanted to telephone *Dada* in Heaven, for she had very frequently talked to him at his office."

Eugene Henry Nichol was born on August 21, 1914 at 5 PM. His baby record was recorded in *Baby's Book*, by Frances Brundage. This is a blue negative photo from his baby book.

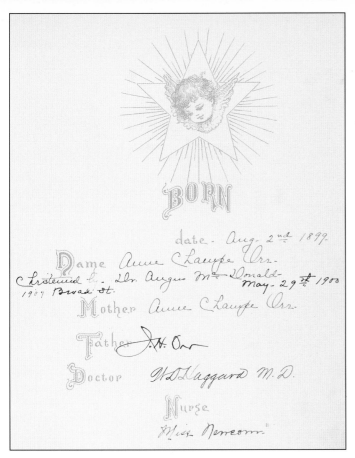

Anne Chawpe Orr was born on August 2, 1899. Her baby record was recorded in *Baby's Book,* by Frances Brundage.

Donald Aberdein Porteous was born on August 3, 1901 at 3:30 PM in San Jacinto, California. His baby record was recorded in *Baby's Biography,* by A.O. Kaplan and illustrated by Frances Brundage. This is his baby picture from the baby book.

Baby: George Henry Percy

Born: Sunday, October 1, 1905 at 8:15 AM in Arlington, Vermont

Father: Nelson B. Percy

Mother: A. B. Percy

Baby Book: *Baby's Biography,* 1891, by A. O. Kaplan with illustrations by Frances Brundage

Comment: A few pages were filled out in George's baby book . On the "Baby Was Given Its First Outing" page we read, "The first lengthy outing was taken Thanksgiving Day 1905, he spent the day with his grandparents in Bennington."

Baby: Donald Aberdein Porteous

Born: Saturday, August 3, 1901 at 3:30 PM in San Jacinto, California

Father: Thomas T. Porteous

Mother: Blanche A, Porteous

Baby Book: *Baby's Biography,* 1891, by A. O. Kaplan with illustrations by Frances Brundage

Comment: Donald's mother completed almost every page, including leaving two locks of hair in the book. Donald attended Washington School on September 27, 1907.

Baby: Betty Ellen Porter

Born: May 5, 1922

Father: A. O. Porter

Mother: Inez Haskins Porter

Baby Book: *Baby's Record, 1891,* by Maud Humphrey

Comment: Betty's baby book is filled with inscriptions and notations plus many baby and family photos. From the "First Outing" page, we read, "Mr. & Mrs. Pheely called for mother and Betty in their machine before lunch, spent the day in their nice cool home." June 21, 1922.

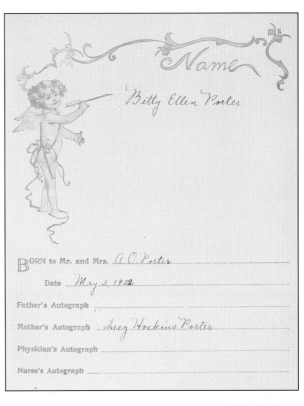

Betty Ellen Porter was born on May 5, 1922. Her baby record was recorded in *Baby's Record,* by Maud Humphrey.

Four family photographs: Betty Porter and family.

Baby: Edna Sallee Poston

Born: October 9, 1903

Baby Book: *Our Baby*, c. 1900, by Will Brundage and Frances Brundage

Comment: Edna's baby book has only a few pages. Each pages has been filled in with a note or two.

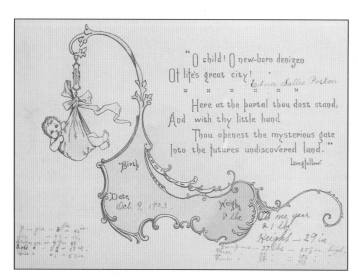

Edna Sallee Poston was born on October 9, 1903. Her baby record was recorded in *Our Baby*, by Will Brundage and Frances Brundage.

Baby: Barbara Wharton Prance

Born: Sunday, November 14, 1926 at 1:30 AM at the Americus and Sumter County Hospital, Americus, Georgia

Parents: Mr. & Mrs. John M. Prance

Baby Book: *Baby's Record Book*, c. 1920, by Josephine Wheeler Weage

Comment: Barbara's baby book was filled to the brim with notes , cards, gift cards pasted in, a lock of hair, and many, many photographs and snapshots. There is even a poem written by her Daddy for her first Birthday.

Baby: Helen Ewart Rome

Born: Sunday, January 25, 1919 at 5:50 PM at Misericordia Hospital, New York City

Father: James Poole Rome

Mother: Henrietta M. Rome

Baby Book: *The New Baby's Biography*, (1891) 1908, by A. O. Kaplan and illustrated by Ruth Mary Hallock and Ysabel De Witte Kaplan

Comment: Helen's baby book was filled with information. On the Addenda page, we read that "Helen is a great talker and never seems to tire."

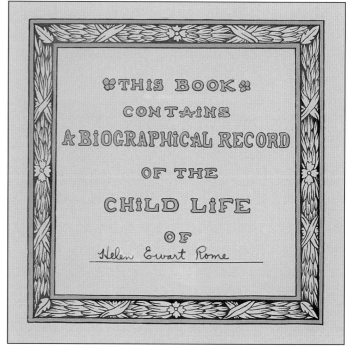

Helen Ewart Rome was born on January 25, 1919 at 5:50 AM at Misericordia Hospital, New York City, New York. Her baby record was recorded in *The New Baby's Biography*, by A. O. Kaplan and illustrated by Ruth Mary Hallock.

Illustrated "Welcome Little Stranger" page: Helen Rome.

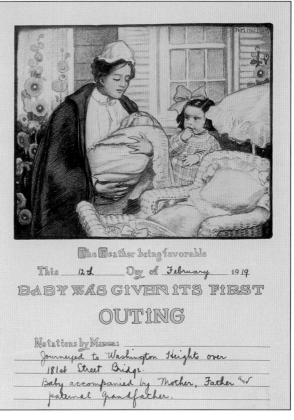

Illustrated "First Outing" page: Helen Rome.

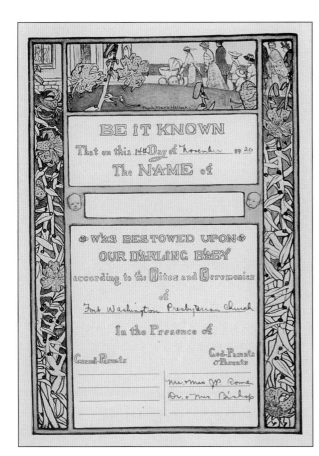

Illustrated "The Name" page: Helen Rome.

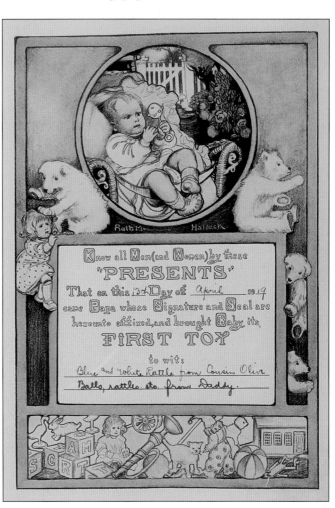

Illustrated "Presents and First Toy" page: Helen Rome.

Illustrated "A Merry Christmas Eve" page: Helen Rome.

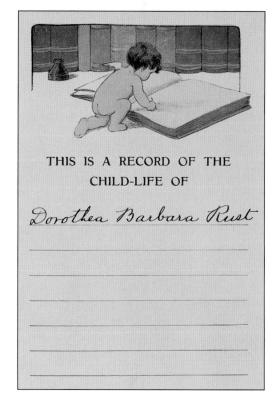

Dorothea Barbara Rust was born on July 21, 1907 at 3:43 AM at Newton Highlands. Her baby records were recorded in *The Biography of Our Baby*, by Edmund Vance Cooke with illustrations by Bessie Collins Pease Gutmann.

Baby: Richard Gridley Roscoe
   Born: April 3, 1909
   Baby Book: *His Majesty The King, Our Baby's Biography*, 1902, by Ethel Elaine Barr
   Comment: Only a few pages were completed in Richard's baby book.

Baby: Dorothea Barbara Rust
   Born: July 21, 1907 at 3:43 AM at Newton Highlands
   Father: William Henry Rust
   Mother: Helen Rust
   Baby Book: *The Biography of Our Baby*, 1906, by Bessie Collins Pease Gutmann
   Comment: In Dorothea's baby book, we found many, many notations and photographs of the baby and her family. On the "Red Letter Day" page, we read, "(she) climbed out of a basket on March 24, 1908."

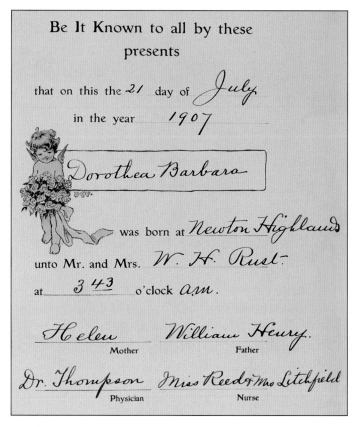

Dorothea Rust: another page of information.

The First Photograph

Taken *Dec 8th 1907* by *Herbert Hall*

Dorothea Rust: Two photographs on "The First Photograph" page: a wonderful picture of baby and father.

Baby: Joseph Lewis Sitnek

Born: March 28, 1915
Father: Jacob Sitnek
Mother: Miriam Graver Sitnek
Baby Book: *Baby's Record,* 1898, by Maud Humphrey

Joseph's baby book was completed page after page. On the "First Outing" page from April 25, 1915: "First ride up to grandma's house on his cart, (he) cried, and had to be brought home."

Baby: Anna Dorothea Sloggett

Born: Thursday, November 19, 1908 at 3:30 PM at Keahua Paia, Maui, Island of Hawaii
Father: Henry Digby Sloggett
Mother: Etta Wilcox Sloggett
Baby Book: *The Biography of Our Baby,* 1906, verses by Edmund Vance Cooke and illustrated by Bessie Collins Pease Gutmann

Comment: On the fly-leaf, it is noted that this book was given to Mother Etta two years prior to Anna's birth.

This is a filled baby book with notes, a lock of hair, and many photographs. On her "Red Letter Day," we found notes dating from 1909 to 1973!

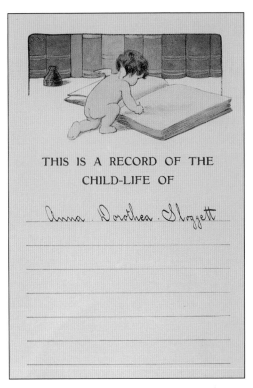

THIS IS A RECORD OF THE CHILD-LIFE OF

Anna Dorothea Sloggett

Anna Dorothea Sloggett was born on Thursday, November 19, 1908 at 3:30 PM at Keahua Paia, Maui, Island of Hawaii. Her baby record was recorded in *The Biography of Our Baby,* by Edmund Vance Cooke with illustrations by Bessie Collins Pease Gutmann.

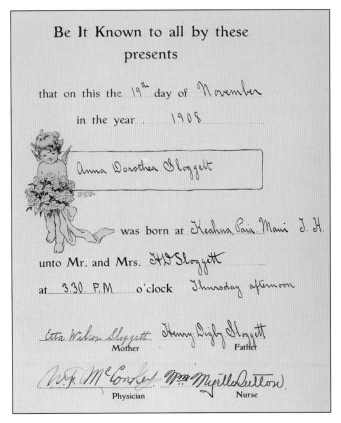

Be It Known to all by these presents

that on this the 19th day of November
in the year 1908

Anna Dorothea Sloggett

was born at *Keahua, Paia, Maui I. H.*
unto Mr. and Mrs. *H D Sloggett*
at *3.30. P.M* o'clock *Thursday afternoon*

Etta Wilcox Sloggett — Mother   *Henry Digby Sloggett* — Father
W. J. McConkey — Physician   *Wm Myrtle Dutton* — Nurse

Anna Sloggett: second page of baby and family information.

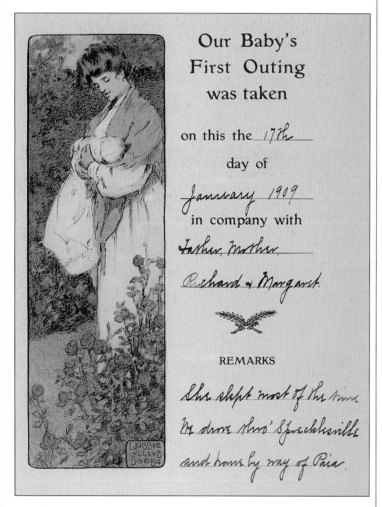

The First Photograph

Taken *at about 3 months* by *Father*

Anna Sloggett: "The First Photograph" page with Anna and her mother.

Our Baby's First Outing was taken

on this the *17th*

day of

January 1909

in company with

Father, Mother,

Richard & Margaret.

REMARKS

She slept most of the time
We drove thro' Spreckelsville
and home by way of Paia

Illustrated "Our Baby's First Outing" page: Anna Sloggett.

Baby: Woodley Bates Smith, Jr.
Born: Sunday, December 21, 1902 at 3:05 PM at the Alexander Maternity Clinic, San Francisco, California
Father: Woodley Bates Smith
Mother: Florence Dresback Smith
Baby Book: *The Baby's Biography,* 1891, by A. O. Kaplan and illustrated by Frances Brundage
Comment: On February 19, 1903, Woodley was taken on his first outing by Aunt Irma and his mother "to Lafayette Square where there were a great many other babies."

Baby: Elizabeth Alberta Spetnager
Born: March 6, 1907 at 3:05 PM
Father: John Madeira Spetnager
Mother: Marie Elizabeth K. Spetnager
Baby Book: *Baby's Book,* c. 1895, by Eda Scott Taylor and illustrated by Frances Brundage
Comment: On Elizabeth's "First Short Clothes" page, we read "June 29, 1907. In celebration of the 42nd wedding anniversary of Grandfather and Grandmother, who were visiting."

Baby: Adelaide Mary Sproehler
Born: 1908, Rochester, New York. She was baptized on January 1, 1909.
Baby Book: *Our Baby,* c. 1900, by Frances Brundage and May Sandheim
Comment: Laid into Adelaide's baby book was a typed list of about fifty gifts, with five dollars in gold from Grandma and Grandpa Sproehler at the top of the list.

Adelaide Mary Sproehler was born in 1908. Her baby record was recorded in *Our Baby,* by Frances Brundage and May Sandheim. This lovely illustrated page tells us that she was baptized in Rochester, New York.

Baby: John Gruwell Stanley, Jr.

Born: September 11, 1916

Parents: Dr. & Mrs. John Gruwell Stanley, dentist

Baby Book: *My Baby's Book*, 1915, by Ella Dolbear Lee and Julia Dyar Hardy with decorations by Ella L. Brison

Comment: The first half of John's baby book was filled in, including three locks of hair and many photographs of baby and family.

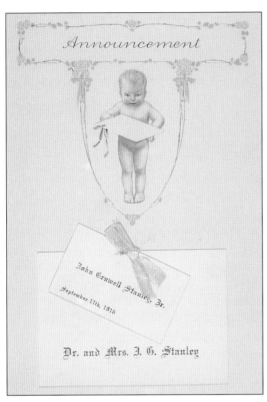

John Gruwell Stanley, Jr., was born on September 11, 1916. His baby record was recorded in *My Baby's Book*, by Ella Dolbear Lee and Julia Hardy. This is the beautiful "Announcement" page with cards pasted in.

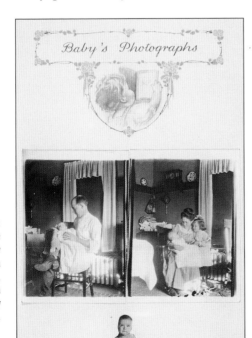

John Stanley, Jr.: two of the wonderful family photographs from his baby book, which is filled with wonderful baby and family history.

Baby: Winifred Carol Storer

Born: Tuesday, August 28, 1917 in Holley, New York

Baby Book: *My Baby's Book*, 1915, by Ella Dolbear Lee and Julia Dyar Hardy with decorations by Ella L. Brison

Comment: The first half of Winifred's baby book has a few notes and a lock of hair.

Baby: Henry Buzzard Sykes

Born: March 22, 1910 at 12:50 AM in Elkhart, Indiana

Father: Walter Avery Sykes

Mother: Maud Buzzard Sykes

Baby Book: *Our Baby*, c. 1900, by Frances Brundage and May Sandheim

Comment: One of Henry's first gifts was $100.00 in telephone stock along with clothes and a rattle. This book is nearly completely filled in, plus notes at the back of the book and a telegram laid in from Carl.

Henry Buzzard Sykes was born on March 22, 1910 in Elkhart, Indiana. His baby information was recorded in *Our Baby*, by Frances Brundage and May Sandheim. His baby book contains many wonderful stories about Henry written by his mother Maud Sykes.

Baby: Eva Stewart Trevelgan

Born: September 30, 1919 at 2:00 at the Riverside Hospital

Father: Edward Trevelgan

Mother: Kathleen Trevelgan

Baby Book: *Our Baby Book,* 1907, by Fanny Y. Cory

Comment: Only a few of pages of Eva's baby book were filled in: a list of gifts and a list of visitors.

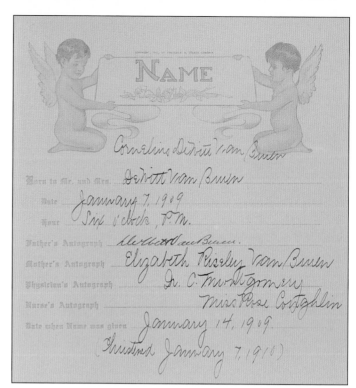

Cornelius Van Buren was born on January 7, 1909. His baby information was recorded in *Baby's History,* by S. D. Runyan.

Eva Stewart Trevelgan was born on September 30, 1919. Her baby record was recorded in *Our Baby Book,* by Fanny Y. Cory. This is the illustrated "Announcement" page.

Baby: Cornelius DeWill Van Buren

Born: January 7, 1909 at 6:00 PM

Father: DeWill Van Buren

Mother: Elizabeth Riseley Van Buren

Baby Book: *Baby's History,* 1908, by S. D. Runyan

Comment: Cornelius's baby book has many notes and records. In February of 1909 his "baby go-cart arrived, he cried like the deuce and didn't like it at all."

Baby: Robert Chaplin Vanderbilt

Born: August 16, 1909 at 12:10 AM

Father: Ralph S. Vanderbilt

Mother: Lillian "Lilly" Vanderbilt

Baby Book: *My Baby's Biography,* c. 1880, by Ida Waugh (without credit)

Comment: His baby book contains a December, 1909 baby photograph. There is a list of baby's presents, baby's first ride on Labor Day of 1910, and a carriage ride with father, mother, and Miss Dumphy.

Baby: Baby Ward

Born: St. Paul, Minnesota

Baby Book: *Our Baby's Record,* 1909, by Sarah K. Smith and Louise Perrett

Comment: This baby book is blank except for the following inscription: "Baby Ward, 477 Portland Ave., St. Paul, MN."

Baby: Muriel Edith Watson

Born: March 19, 1902 at 10:50 PM

Baby Book: *All About Baby,* c. 1900

Comment: Muriel was born at 6 Albion Road, Scarborough.

Muriel Edith Watson was born on March 19, 1902 at 10:50 PM. Her baby information is contained in *All About Baby*.

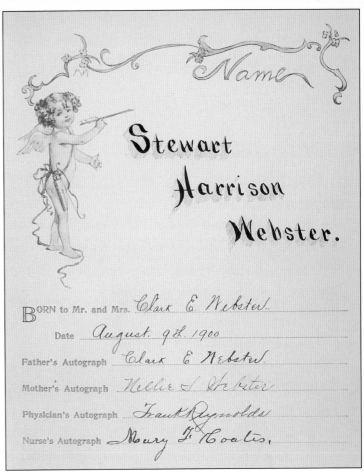

Stewart Harrison Webster was born on August 9, 1900 in Syracuse, New York. His baby information was recorded in *Baby's Record*, by Maud Humphrey.

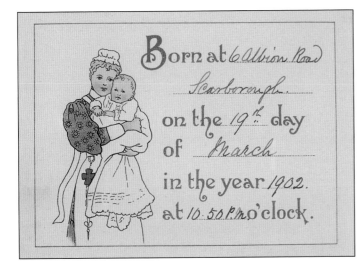

Muriel Watson: her "Born at" page.

Baby: Stewart Harrison Webster
 Born: August 9, 1900 at Syracuse, New York
 Father: Clark E. Webster
 Mother: Nellie S. Webster
 Baby Book: *Baby's Record*, 1898, by Maud Humphrey
 Comment: Stewart's baby book was a gift from "his Papa." Nearly every page has a note or notation plus several baby photograph and a lock of his hair.

Stewart Webster: his first "Large Photograph."

Baby: Louis Alan Welch

    Born: June 23, 1907 at 4:25 PM

    Father: Louis Welch

    Mother: Ethel Welch

    Baby Book: *The Biography of Our Baby,* 1906, verses by Edmund Vance Cooke and illustrations by Bessie Collins Pease Gutmann

    Comment: Only a few pages in Louis's baby book have any notes.

Baby: Barbara Marguerita Wilkin

    Born: Wednesday, November, 1916 at 3:51 AM in Graymount, Belfast, Ireland

    Father: I. Z. Wilkin

    Mother: Elfrida B. Wilkin

    Baby Book: *Baby's Souvenir,* c. 1910, by A. O. Kaplan and illustrated by Frances Brundage

    Comment: About a third of Barbara's baby book has notes and there are several wonderful photographs.

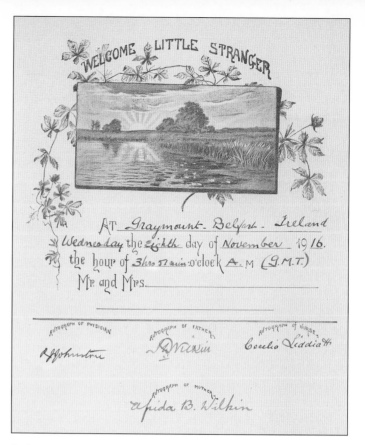

Barbara Wilkin: "Welcome Little Stranger" page.

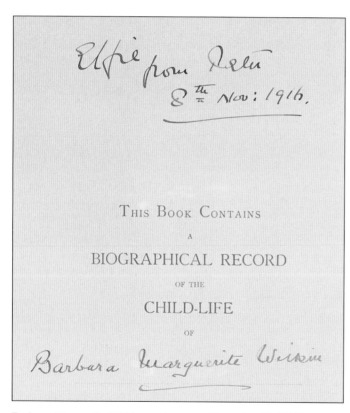

Barbara Marguerita Wilkin was born on November 8, 1916 in Belfast, Ireland. Her baby record was recorded in *Baby's Souvenir,* by A. O. Kaplan and illustrated by Frances Brundage.

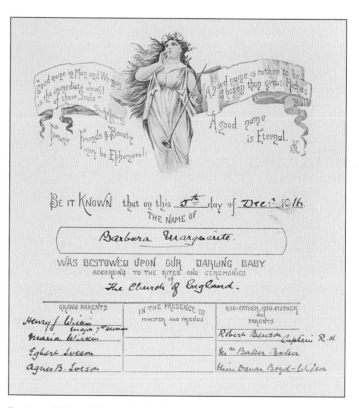

Barbara Wilkin: "Named and Christened" page.

Barbara
Sept: 1919

Barbara Wilkin: her photograph on September, 1919.

Baby: Frances Alice Woodworth

Born: Saturday, July 9, 1892 at 2:10 AM at Seneca, Nemaha County, Kansas

Parents: Judge & Mrs. Samuel Woodworth

Baby Book: *The Baby's Biography,* 1891, by A. O. Kaplan and illustrated by Frances Brundage

One of Frances's first presents was "a silver spoon lined with gold from Aunt Maggie Treat of Tucson, Arizona Territory." Around Christmas time, grandma Woodworth sent a her a silver mug.

Baby: Unknown Baby in Toronto, Canada

Baby Book: *The Biography of Our Baby,* 1906, verses by Edmund Vance Cook and illustrations by Bessie Collins Pease Gutmann

At the back of this blank baby book, we have six pages filled with signatures of people who attended the baby's May 8, 1920 Christening Day. The Toronto bookseller from whom the book was purchased wrote the following on his invoice: "The names at the back are for the most part Blue-Bloods of Toronto Society, et. al. For example, the Eaton Family was a famous Canadian Department Store Empire."

Chapter Four

Alphabetical List of Baby Books With Price Guide

Some baby books have one title on the cover and a different title on the title page. In addition, if the book came in a box, the box might have still a third title. The titles of baby books are very similar to one another, in some cases even identical. Some baby books have split titles and may be listed under two titles, each one being correct.

The price of a baby book will vary time after time. Old illustrated children's books have a wide price range. The collectible illustrators are highly sought after by collectors of illustrated children's books, who sometimes include baby books as part of their collections. Generally, the condition of a baby book and who the illustrator is will dictate the seller's price, not whether or not the baby book has been "used" by the owner. We offer our pricing guide based on average to very good condition.

Some of the books were printed with more than one cover or the same cover with different colored fabrics and/or different colored lettering. As noted, some baby books were sold in a box. If the box is decorated and in good repair, this feature will add 20% to the value. A few books were published with a dust wrap or book jacket; this feature will add value, too.

All About Baby, c. 1890, no author, no illustrator, no publisher. $75-125.

All About Me (cover), *All About Me, Baby's Record* (title page), 1918, by Josephine Wheeler Weage. The Saalfield Publishing Company. Blue cover with color illustration. $75-125.

Baby, c. 1890. No author, no illustrator, no publisher. $75-125.

Baby, by Meta Morris Grimball, 1915 edition has no stated publisher; the 1921 edition was published by Cupples & Leon Company. Covers in blue/green, pink, and moiré silk with gold embossed lettering. $100-200.

Baby Book, A Record of Our Baby, 1921, by Meta Morris Grimball. Cupples & Leon Company. $75-150.

Baby Days, A Sunbonnet Record, 1910, by Bertha L. Corbett. Rand, McNally. Blue and pink covers with gold and white embossed designs, watered moiré silk, and gold textured silk with gold and lavender embossed imprint. $125-250.

Baby Days, Our Baby's History, 1880, by Amy Neally with illustrations by Ida Waugh, Eddie Andrews, and Harriett M. Bennett. Dutton Publishers. $100-250.

Baby Dear (cover), *A Record of Sunny Hours*, 1926, no author or illustrator. Published by Richard G. Krueger, Inc. $50-100.

Babyhood Days, 1915, by Jessie Alma Pierson with frontispiece by Evelyn von Hartmann. Barse & Hopkins Publishers. Pink fabric cover with embossed gold. $75-150.

Baby Mine, 1920, by Fanny Y. Cory. Brown & Bigelow Publishers. Soft cover. $125-250.

Baby-Mine (cover), *Baby's Book of Events* (title page), c. 1920, by Queen Holden. Richard G. Krueger Inc. Padded moiré silk cover with hand painted decoration. $75-150.

Baby's Biography, 1891 and 1913, by A. O. Kaplan with illustrations by Frances Brundage. Book covers include: (1) ivory fabric with navy blue lettering and balloon in red, (2) ivory fabric with gold and navy embossed lettering, (3) tan and blue fabric with balloon in red and gold lettering, (4) blue fabric with navy blue embossed lettering, (5) red cloth with black embossed lettering, and (6) red and tan cloth cover with gold embossed lettering and the balloon in black. Brentano's Publishers. $150-300.

Baby's Biography, 1913, by Clara M. Burd. Published by Foster Brothers Manufacturing Co. Cover has pasted on color illustration and gold lettering. $75-150.

Baby's Book, c. 1910, by Cornelia Morton Weyburn with verses by Francis Buzzell. Barse & Hopkins Publishers. Covers in blue fabric, pink fabric, and silk with gold embossed lettering. $75-150.

Baby's Book, c. 1905 by Frances Brundage and M. Bowley. Published by Raphael Tuck & Sons. Pale blue cover with gold embossed lettering. $150-300.

Baby's Book, c. 1900, by Ida Taylor Scott with illustrations by Frances Brundage. Raphael Tuck and Sons Publishers. Book covers: (1) green cloth with gold embossed lettering, (2) blue cloth with gold embossed lettering, (3) blue cloth with pink/gold flower and gold embossed lettering, (4) padded silk in several versions. $150-300.

Baby's Book, A Record, 1916, by Florence Choate and Elizabeth Curtis. Published by Frederick A. Stokes Company. Blue and pink covers. $50-100.

Baby's Childhood Days, c. 1920, by Dulah Evans Krehbiel. Published by Reilly & Britton Co. $50-125.

Baby's Diary, c. 1890, by Henrietta Willebeek Le Mair. Published by Augener, Ltd. White hard cover with color picture pasted into circle with gold embossed lettering. $200-450.

Baby's History, 1890, by S. D. Runyan. Frederick A. Stokes Co. Publishers. Blue cover with blue and silver embossed design and lettering. $100-250.

Baby's Journal, c. 1880, by S. Alice Bray. Published by Anson D. F. Randolph & Company. Covers include three different designs: (1) doctor, nurse, baby and scales, (2) title on diagonal with baby and wild flowers, and (3) title on horizontal with baby and flowers. $50-150.

Baby's Own Book, 1910, by Clara Powers Wilson. Published by the Reilly & Lee Company. Pink and blue fabric covers. $50-100.

Baby's Own Book, 1923, by N. Farini. No publisher. $50-150.

Baby's Own Book, c. 1910, no author, no illustrator, no publisher. $50-100.

Baby's Record, 1898, by Maud Humphrey. Book covers: (1) decorated in flowers and gold lettering, (2) blue fabric, (3) green fabric with silver lettering, (4) white fabric with silver lettering, and (5) grey fabric with silver lettering. Number of full page color illustrations: twelve pages, three pages, and one page editions. Published by Frederick A. Stokes Company. $300-500.

Baby's Record, 1920 and 1928, by Anne Anderson. Pink cover with gold embossed lettering. George Harrop & Co. $125-250.

Baby's Record, c. 1915, by Clara M. Burd. Published by the G. F. Fitzgerald & Co. $75-175.

Baby's Record Book (cover), *Our Baby* (title page), 1918, by Josephine Wheeler Weage. The Saalfield Publishing Company. Dark blue cover with silver embossed lettering. $75-125.

Baby's Red Letter Days, 1901, by Jessie Wilcox Smith. Book covers: (1) embossed pictorial and (2) embossed tan. Published by Just Foods Co. $125-250.

Baby's Souvenir, c. 1910, by A. O. Kaplan with illustrations by Frances Brundage. Book covers: (1) combination blue moiré silk with beige cloth and (2) striped with polka-dots, moiré silk with gold embossed lettering. (Both covers have Brundage spelled Brondage.) Published by Dean & Sons. $200-400.

Biography of Our Baby, 1906, by Edmund Vance Cooke with illustrations by Bessie Collins Pease Gutmann. Book covers: (1) white gilt and pictorial cloth, (2) light blue fabric, and (3) pink fabric. Published by Dodge & Co. $125-250.

Book of Baby Mine, 1915, by Melcena Burns Denny. Published by the Simplicity Company. Covers are in (1) smooth leather or (2) rough leather with embossing. $50-150.

Dear Baby, c. 1920. No author, no illustrator, no publisher. $50-100.

Flower Song, 1930, by Carlyle Emery. Von Hoffman Press. Soft cover, string tied. $75-150.

His Majesty, The King, Our Baby's Biography, 1902, by Ethel Elaine Barr. Published by George M. Hill Co. $75-150.

Little Baby's Big Days, 1916, by Edith Truman Woolf. Published by C. R. Gibson & Co. $75-150.

Mother Stork's Baby Book, 1904, by Albertine Randall Wheelan. The Dodge Publishing Co. $100-200.

My Biography, 1914, by J. C. Powers and W. E. Powers. Published by Borden's Condensed Milk Co. $50-125.

My Baby's Biography, c. 1880, illustrated by Ida Waugh (without credit). Published by Ernest Nister and E. P. Dutton & Co. $100-250.

My Baby's Book, 1915, by Ella Dolbear Lee and Julia Hardy with illustrations by Ella L. Brison. Book covers: (1) pink/white striped fabric, (2) blue fabric, and (3) pink fabric. Published by P. F. Volland & Co. $175-400.

My Baby's Book, 1927, by E. Schacherer. Book covers: (1) children at play and (2) baby with garland. Published by Laird & Lee. $75-150.

New Baby's Biography, 1891 & 1908, by A. O. Kaplan with illustrations by Ruth Mary Hallock and Ysabel DeWitte Kaplan. Cloth covers in blue, pink, and white. Published by Brentano's. $200-400.

Our Baby, 1903, by Frances Brundage and Will Brundage. Published by C. R. Gibson & Co. $150-250.

Our Baby, 1909, by Frances Brundage and May Sandheim. Book covers: (1) blue fabric with silver embossed lettering, (2) pink fabric with silver embossed lettering, and (3) padded silk. Published by Raphael Tuck & Sons. $150-250.

Our Baby, 1927, by Queen Holden. Padded blue moiré silk. Published by Richard G. Krueger. $75-150.

Our Baby, c. 1920, by Matilda Gray. Gray & White Publishing Co., Salem Oregon. Beige cover, string tied. $50-125.

Our Baby, c. 1900, no author, no illustrator, no publisher. $50-100.

Our Baby (cover), *Baby* (title page), 1915, by Meta Morris Grimball. No publisher. Moiré silk cover. $100-200.

Our Baby, A History, c. 1910. by Josephine Bruce. No publisher. $100-150.

Our Baby Book, 1907, by Fanny Y. Cory. Pink or blue fabric cover. Bobbs-Merrill Company. $100-250.

Our Baby's Early Days, 1908, by Bessie Pease Gutmann and Meta Morris Grimball. Blue fabric cover. Best & Company. $200-400.

Our Baby's Journal, c. 1910, by Helen P. Strong. No publisher. White moiré silk cover. $75-150.

Our Baby's Record, 1909, by Sarah K. Smith and Louise Perrett. Dodge Publishing Co. $75-125.

Record of Our Baby, 1921, by Meta Morris Grimball. Pink cover with gold embossed lettering. Cupples & Leon Company. $125-200.

Record of Our Baby, c. 1895, by Ida Waugh (without credit). Covers in blue fabric and pink fabric. Published by E. P. Dutton & Co. $50-100.

Record of Our Baby's Life, 1912, by Albertine Randall Wheelan. Soft tan cover embossed with gold lettering. Dodge Publishing Company. $75-150.

Story of Our Baby, 1929, by Edith Kovor. No stated publisher. Soft cover. $50-100.

When I Was A Baby, c. 1905, by Helen P. Strong. Moiré silk cover. $100-200.